PROVOKING EXPLOITS

through the Force of

IMPOSING AGGRESSIVE FAITH

GLENN AREKION

Faith House Publishing

ISBN 978-1-943282-07-4

faithhousepublishing.com

Printed in the United States of America

Second Edition 2018

CONTENTS

INTRODUCTION

ALL through the bible, you will see men and women who had great exploits in their lives due to their faith. Abraham, David, Jacob, Elijah, Daniel, Deborah and Anna are some examples. David killed a giant by the name of Goliath; Daniel shut the mouths of lions; the three Hebrew boys, Meshach, Shadrach and Abed-nego walked through the fire without being burnt as the fourth man showed up. In this book we will look at the secrets of their exploits and appropriate them into our lives. Our foundational text will be from the book of Daniel:

And such as do wickedly against the covenant shall he corrupt by flatteries: but the people that do know their God shall be strong, and do exploits.
DANIEL 11:32

We will look briefly at the history of this verse and then look at how we can apply the demands of this verse to provoke unlimited exploits in our lives. One thing we must realize is that even though God wants us to have great exploits they do not come automatically. If exploits came automatically after being saved then all believers would be walking in divine exploits. This is not the case. Now, everybody *can* have exploits but not everyone does because there are some things lacking in our arsenal.

You will quickly discover that what brings exploits into your life is faith. What kind of faith? Not the passive kind of faith that the majority of the church world is into, but imposing, aggressive faith that will not take no for an answer. As you go through the pages of this book, you will get an understanding of faith like never before. It has been there in the Bible all along, we just did not have the guts to preach or teach it. Some have taught on it and have been criticized for being extreme or hyper faith. I will show

Scriptures after Scriptures to get you into imposing, aggressive faith that manifests exploits. God loves it when we corner Him with our faith, and when we do so He comes out swinging. When God swings He never misses. After reading this book your faith will be charged and strong enough to reel in the exploits that you are looking for. We will look at five requirements to provoke unlimited exploits and they are:

❖ Knowing God.
❖ Being strong.
❖ Having Imposing, aggressive faith.
❖ Persistent and importunate prayer.
❖ The leading of the Spirit.

You are called to a life of exploits but if you are weak the devil will exploit you. Only the strong in faith have great exploits. The choice is yours: you can either be weak in faith and be exploited by the devil or be strong in faith and bully the devil.

❖ Imposing, aggressive faith secures exploits.
❖ Imposing, aggressive faith is dominant over the world, the flesh and the devil.
❖ Imposing, aggressive faith bullies the devil and circumstances instead of being bullied by the devil and circumstances.
❖ Imposing, aggressive faith takes charge.

A life of exploits awaits you! Are you ready?

CHAPTER 1
CALLED TO DO GREAT EXPLOITS

And such as do wickedly against the covenant shall he corrupt by flatteries:
but the people that do know their God shall be strong, and do exploits.
                                                          DANIEL 11:32

There are no doubts about it! God has called you to a life of great exploits.
When we look through the Old and New Testaments we see a litany of
ordinary men and women who did impossible feats through undaunted faith
that made the enemies of life bow before them. For sure as a believer you
have the same faith, same Word, same Holy Spirit, same name of Jesus and
the same calling upon your life. Peter, in his epistle said that God has called
you to a life of glory and virtue and this is why He gave you his exceeding
precious promises to enable you to outwardly express the divine nature
deposited in your spirit (2 Peter 1:3-4). You do not need to go through life
hearing great testimonies of other people yet never having one for yourself.

For so many believers the testimonies of breakthroughs in their lives
are sporadic, if ever. In fact for the majority of believers, the time between
miracles and exploits can be years which does not seem to bother them.
Many are satisfied to go through life with the mindset, 'Well I know Jesus as
my Lord and I know I'm on my way to heaven. It will all be worthwhile when
I get to heaven.' While this is great news that you are on your way to heaven,
why settle only for the sweet by-and-by when you can taste unlimited exploits
while you are on the earth? Yes you read it right! You can have unlimited
exploits while you are alive on this side of heaven. The Psalmist declared,
'Blessed be the Lord, who daily loadeth us with benefits, even the God of our
salvation. Selah.' (Psalm 68:19). You can have daily exploits. It's in your
Bible! There is no need to have a huge gap between exploits. In this book
I deliberately want to rouse your faith – which is the most potent force in the

universe – to overcome any challenge that the enemy throws your way. It is through imposing, aggressive faith that you will provoke unlimited exploits. The Webster's Dictionary defines *exploit* as a notable or heroic act and an exciting feat. Therefore as you begin to tap into unlimited exploits you will see notable feats that will be an exciting adventure in your life. Right from the get-go I want to drive into you the notion that provoking exploits will be done by faith. Those who obtained a good report in Hebrews 11 and throughout the Bible did so by aggressive faith, which triggered legendary feats upon the earth, defying death and the devil. Your good report of great exploits will be as a result of militant, dominant and imposing faith.

ô Brief History

Going back to our beginning verse from the book of Daniel, '*And such as do wickedly against the covenant shall he corrupt by flatteries: but the people that do know their God shall be strong, and do exploits*' (Daniel 11:32), we need to look at the history of this verse in order for us to grasp what Daniel was prophesying. The tiny book of Daniel, consisting of twelve chapters, is one of the most hated books by liberal theologians and professors. For years they have been trying to discredit the authorship and the book because it is so accurate in its prophecies. Some have tried to say that Daniel was not the author, it had to be someone else who wrote the history after it occurred because to them nobody could so accurately predict the future. Jesus debunked this theory as He verified Daniel's authorship in his sermon:

> *When ye therefore shall see the abomination of desolation, spoken of by Daniel the prophet, stand in the holy place, (whoso readeth, let him understand)*
>
> MATTHEW 24:15

The first six chapters of the book of Daniel deal with history as it happened to Daniel: the captivity, Nebuchadnezzar and Babylon. The following six chapters deal with visions and prophecies of successive world empires. The reason why liberal scholars hate it so much is because Daniel precisely predicted all the world empires, the events during Intertestamental times (also known as the Silent Period) to the end times events that we are seeing today. So let's focus on our foundational verse, the first part:

And such as do wickedly against the covenant shall he corrupt by flatteries...

A brief history of the fulfillment of this verse is referring to Antiochus Epiphanes, also known as Antiochus IV (c.215–163 bc), son of Antiochus III. Historically he is the one responsible for the term 'abomination of desolation' in the Bible (Daniel 11:31). He erected the statue of Zeus on his birthday in the temple of God in the Holy of Holies which was an abomination, forbidding the daily morning and evening sacrifices, instead he sacrificed pigs on the altar. He believed that he was the incarnation of Zeus and this is why he called himself Antiochus Epiphanes meaning *a manifestation of the divine*. In his attempt to hellenize the Jews, Antiochus also:

❖ Brought prostitutes into the temple.
❖ Introduced idolatry.
❖ Forbade the reading of the Scriptures and the observance of the Sabbath.
❖ Interdicted the circumcision.
❖ Killed and sold thousands of the resistant Jews to coerce the rest of the nation to renounce Jehovah God.

However these abominable actions resulted in the revival of Jewish nationalism and the exploits of the Maccabean revolt. Although he referred to himself as Antiochus Epiphanes – supposedly as an incarnation of Zeus – he became known as Antiochus Epimanes meaning Antiochus the madman.

The second part of the prophecy, '*but the people that do know their God shall be strong and do exploits*' was fulfilled by Judas Maccabeus who, with a few fully dedicated dissidents, revolted, resisted, attacked and defeated the evil plans of Antiochus Epiphanes. Before each battle encounter he would rouse and stir his men, who became known as Maccabees (from the Hebrew word meaning 'hammer') to willingly fight to die for the cause of God. The exploits of these men became legendary, which resulted in the rededication of the temple, the removal of the statue, the reinstating of the daily sacrifices with a new altar and the rebuilding of the wall. The Jewish festival of Hanukah is a commemoration of the Maccabee's restoration of Jewish worship in the temple in Jerusalem in 165BC.

Your good report of great exploits will be as a result of militant, dominant and imposing faith

---

Now I want to insert and highlight from two brief commentaries, the Barnes and Benson Bible Commentaries' to give you an even better understanding of what was happening in this verse in order to see how we can provoke exploits. They both also pulled information from other historical books which are not in the Bible but nevertheless gave us the history of the day.

And such as do wickedly against the covenant – That is, among the Jews. They who apostatized, and who became willing to receive the religion of foreigners. There "was" such a party in Jerusalem, and it was numerous. See Jahn, "Heb. Commonwealth," pp. 258, 259. Compare 1 Macc. 1:52: "Then many of the people were gathered unto them, to wit, every one that forsook the law; and so they committed evils in the land."

Shall he corrupt by flatteries – By flattering promises of his favor, of office, of national prosperity... See the notes at Daniel 11:21. The margin is, "or, cause to dissemble." The meaning of the Hebrew word חָנֵף chânêph is, rather, "to profane, to pollute, to defile;" and the idea here is, that he would cause them to become defiled; that is, that he would seduce them to impiety and apostasy.

But the people that do know their God – They who adhere to the service and worship of the true God, and who are incapable of being seduced to apostasy and sin. The reference here is, undoubtedly, to Judas Maccabeus and his followers– a full account of whose doings is to be found in the books of the Maccabees. See also Prideaux, "Con." iii. 245, following, and Jahn, "Heb. Commonwealth," pp. 268, following.

Shall be, strong – Shall evince great valor, and shall show great vigour in opposing him.

And do exploits – The word "exploits," as in Daniel 11:28, is supplied by the translators, but not improperly. The meaning is, **that they would show great prowess, and perform illustrious deeds in battle**. See Prideaux, "Con." iii. pp. 262, 263.

ALBERT BARNES NOTES ON THE BIBLE

Daniel 11:32. Such as do wickedly shall he corrupt by flatteries – This is a declaration, that there would be many wicked persons who would be enticed to this idolatry by Antiochus's persuasions. Jason and Menelaus, who were made high-priests by Antiochus for a sum of money, afterward became his instruments, and consented to the setting up of this idol: see 1Ma 1:52; 2Ma 4:13-15; and 2Ma 5:15; and 2Ma 6:21.

But the people that do know their God – That are savingly acquainted with him, and adhere to his true worship and service.

Shall be strong and do exploits – **When others yield to the tyrant's demands, and surrender their consciences to his impositions, these shall bravely keep their ground, resist the temptation, and make the tyrant himself ashamed of his attempt upon them.** Good old Eleazar, one of the principal scribes, was one of these, rather choosing to suffer torments and death than defile himself by eating any thing unclean: see 2 Maccabees 6:19. The mother and her seven sons resolutely adhered to their religion, though they knew they must be put to death for so doing, 2 Maccabees 7. This might well be called doing exploits; for to choose to suffer rather than to sin is a great exploit. And it was by being strong in faith that they did those exploits; and bore to be tortured, not accepting deliverance, as the apostle speaks, Hebrews 11:25. "And many in Israel were fully resolved and confirmed in themselves not to eat any thing unclean, whereupon they chose rather to die, that they might not be defiled with meats, and that they might not profane the holy covenant," 1Ma 1:62-63. Or, it may refer to the military courage and achievements of Judas Maccabeus and others, in opposition to Antiochus. Observe, reader, the right knowledge of God is and will be the strength of the soul, and through it gracious persons do exploits. They that know his name will put their trust in him, and by that trust will do great things.

JOSEPH BENSON BIBLE COMMENTARY

When others yield to the tyrant's demands, and surrender their consciences to his impositions, these shall bravely keep their ground, resist the temptation, and make the tyrant himself ashamed of his attempt

Now that you have a brief understanding of the history behind this verse, we can move on to what we want to get our teeth into, 'Provoking unlimited exploits'. Different translations of this verse read as follows:

'Those that be knowing their God will be valiant showing great prowess and perform illustrious deeds in battle.'

'...but the people that know their God shall prevail and succeed.'

DRB

You have to have this resolve in your mind that you will perform illustrious deeds in battle; that, no matter what you go through and how many come against you, you will prevail and succeed. Notice the commentary of Joseph Benson, *'When others yield to the tyrant's demands, and surrender their consciences to his impositions, these shall bravely keep their ground, resist the temptation, and make the tyrant himself ashamed of his attempt upon them.'* May that become a reality in your life! You will not yield, bow and surrender to the tyrannies of Satan. You will be so charged with imposing and militant faith that whenever the devil attacks, you will uproot his devices and tell him, 'Shame on you devil'.

CHAPTER 2
THE DEMANDS FOR PROVOKING
UNLIMITED EXPLOITS

And such as do wickedly against the covenant shall he corrupt by flatteries:
but the people that do know their God shall be strong, and do exploits.

DANIEL 11:32

EXPLOITS are not automatic just because you become a born-again believer. If it were so, then all believers would be experiencing exploits. Instead, as you know, there are literally millions of believers who are exploited by circumstances rather than doing great exploits. If you believe, like many ill-informed believers, 'Well, if the Lord wants me to have exploits, then I will,' this is exactly the attitude possessed by people who never have any exploits; and you won't either. A lackadaisical, lackluster and listless attitude is one that will *be exploited* rather than *do exploits*. Therefore you need to understand that there are some demands in order for you to provoke unlimited exploits.

A lackadaisical, lackluster and listless attitude is one that
will be exploited rather than one that does exploits

From our verse from the book of Daniel, it is explicitly clear that there are demands necessary to provoke unlimited exploits. We are told, '*the people that do know their God shall be strong and do exploits.*' So here are two requirements and demands to do exploits:

❖ Know Their God.
❖ Be Strong.

Knowing God and being strong are vital attributes for exploits. These are not automatic. Not everybody who is born-again knows God and certainly not every one who is born-again is strong, even though they should be; there are no valid excuses to be weak, with all the information available to us today. There are some born-again believers who are just as ignorant about God as some unbelievers. There are some who walk in unbelief just as unbelievers do. There are some believers who would not recognize God if He was walking down the street with a red shirt and red cap on.

We will look at these two requirements mentioned above. Then, of course Hebrews 11, which is the *exploits* chapter, makes it abundantly clear that faith is a major ingredient to provoke supernatural feats. Let me reiterate: it is not passive faith but imposing, aggressive violent faith that possesses the promises of God; it is the kind of faith that imposes, superimposes and opposes; it is the kind of faith that will oppose and bully the devil; it is the kind of faith that will intimidate devils; it is the God-kind of faith that Jesus displayed in His earthly walk. It is also the God kind of faith that Paul expressed on his missionary journeys and adventures. We will imitate Jesus and Paul to intimidate the devil. Fourthly, we will look at *persistent and importunate prayer* to possess your possessions. Too many believers pray passionless and perfunctory prayers that amount to nothing. Importunate praying is the releasing mechanism of your imposing faith. We will define importunate prayer and look at examples in the Scriptures. Fifthly, we will look at the importance of being led by the Spirit, which is a major cause of provoking exploits. It is written of our Lord Jesus, '*he was led by the Spirit... and he returned in the power of the Spirit*' (Luke 4:1,14). When you are led by the Spirit, you become a major problem for the devil. It is the right of every believer to be led by the Spirit. It is not only for a special preacher but for you too. The Holy Spirit is our advocate, comforter, counselor, helper, intercessor, strengthener and standby power. Once you hear from the Holy Spirit, aggressive faith – able to take hold of your blessing – is activated and the rest will be the writing of your history.

---

*Too many believers pray passionless and perfunctory
prayers that do not amount to anything*

So the five things that we will look at are:

❖ Knowing God.

❖ Being strong.

❖ Aggressive and imposing faith.

❖ Exploits through Persistence and Importunate Prayer.

❖ Exploits through the leading of the Spirit.

---

*Imposing, aggressive faith is the kind of faith that will oppose and
bully the devil. It is the kind of faith that will intimidate the devil*

**If you are interested in doing unlimited exploits and tired of being
exploited by the devil then let the adventure into greatness begin.**

CHAPTER 3
KNOWING GOD TO DO GREAT EXPLOITS

IT will take knowing God to provoke unlimited exploits. The believer who knows God is the believer who will know breakthroughs. The man who knows God will know the futility of the devil. If you ever catch a glimpse of the *omnipotence* of God you will understand the *impotence* of the devil, demons and witches. This is why the devil fights hard against you knowing God. The prophet Isaiah opens our perspective on Satan in his writing:

> *How art thou fallen from heaven, O Lucifer, son of the morning! how art thou cut down to the ground, which didst weaken the nations! For thou hast said in thine heart, I will ascend into heaven, I will exalt my throne above the stars of God: I will sit also upon the mount of the congregation, in the sides of the north: I will ascend above the heights of the clouds; I will be like the most High. Yet thou shalt be brought down to hell, to the sides of the pit. **They that see thee shall narrowly look upon thee, and consider thee, saying, Is this the man that made the earth to tremble, that did shake kingdoms; That made the world as a wilderness, and destroyed the cities thereof; that opened not the house of his prisoners?** All the kings of the nations, even all of them, lie in glory, every one in his own house.*
>
> ISAIAH 14:12-18

Isaiah reveals that we will look at the devil and wonder what the fuss was all about. You don't have to wait that long in the future, you can have the same sentiment today as you look at him from your elevated position in heavenly places in Christ Jesus and from the perspective of the Word. What others tremble at, you will laugh at because you know God. When you know God you are emboldened and act like Him.

❖ Knowing God makes the devil a zero factor in your life.

❖ Knowing the supremacy of God exposes the deficiency of the devil.

❖ Knowing the superiority of God enables you to see the inferiority of the devil.

❖ Knowing the greatness of God unveils the smallness of the devil.

❖ Knowing the omnipotence of God reveals the impotence of the devil.

From generations to generations, ungodly men have endeavored to eradicate the existence of God from society. We saw this playing out in communist nations and it's being played out in today's liberal nations, with liberal politicians, the liberal media and liberal stars who want to make themselves god over society with no morality. What is God's response?

*Why do the heathen rage, and the people imagine a vain thing? The kings of the earth set themselves, and the rulers take counsel together, against the Lord, and against his anointed, saying, Let us break their bands asunder, and cast away their cords from us. **He that sitteth in the heavens shall laugh: the Lord shall have them in derision.** Then shall he speak unto them in his wrath, and vex them in his sore displeasure.*

PSALM 2:1-5

Your present exposure to God will determine your future exploits

---

While the heathens are raging against God, He is laughing at them. God never panics or gets flustered when kings and leaders of this world rage against Him. Why? Because He is God. Voltaire, the famous French philosopher despised God and said, 'One hundred years from today the Bible will be a forgotten book.' Voltaire is gone but the Bible is still here! After his death, for nearly 100 years, his house in Geneva was used as the storehouse for the Bible Society which sold Bibles out of his house! Today it is a museum. God will not be mocked. Communist China and Russia endeavored to remove every trace of God from society and yet today there are more Christians in China than in America. God always has the last word. This is why you must know God and good will follow.

> *Acquaint now thyself with him, and be at peace: thereby good shall come unto thee. Receive, I pray thee, the law from his mouth, and lay up his words in thine heart. If thou return to the Almighty, thou shalt be built up, thou shalt put away iniquity far from thy tabernacles. Then shalt thou lay up gold as dust, and the gold of Ophir as the stones of the brooks. Yea, the Almighty shall be thy defence, and thou shalt have plenty of silver.*
>
> JOB 22:21-25

Once you catch a glimpse of the omnipotence of God you will understand the impotence of the devil, demons and witches

---

Knowing God

The greatest thing you can ever learn is how to know God and be close to Him, just like John was. While everyone wondered who the betrayer was, John, who had his head on the chest of Jesus, found out who the culprit was (John 13:21-26). The great apostle Paul revealed his passion, '*That I may know him and the power of his resurrection*' (Philippians 3:10). The question remains, 'How do I know God?' I am going to give you four sure ways to know God. There are, of course, more ways to know God but these four will be the strong foundations that you need.

❖ The Written Word.
❖ People over and around you.
❖ Communion of the Holy Spirit.
❖ Church attendance.

ê Knowing God through The Written Word

The number one way you get to know God is through and by His Word. The Bible is the revelation of God to mankind and more specifically to you. I love what Smith Wigglesworth said many years ago, 'I understand God by His Word. I cannot understand God by impressions or feelings; I cannot get to know God by sentiments. If I am going to know God, I am going to know Him by His Word.' You can't go around this fact. If you want to know God you must develop a relationship with your Bible. It is not just a book to carry but it is God speaking to you. Look at the words of Job:

> *Acquaint now thyself with him, and be at peace: thereby good shall come unto thee. Receive, I pray thee, the law from his mouth, and lay up his words in thine heart.*
>
> JOB 22:21, 22

Job then showed us how we get acquainted with him. He said, '*Receive, I pray thee, the law from his mouth, and lay up his words in thine heart.*' You get acquainted with God when you receive the words of his mouth. Jesus said, '*Man shall not live by bread alone, but by every word that proceedeth out of the mouth of God*' (Matthew 4:4). Job also said, '*My foot hath held his steps, his way have I kept, and not declined. Neither have I gone back from the commandment of his lips; I have esteemed the words of his mouth more than my necessary food*' (Job 23:11-12). We must develop a greater appetite for the knowledge of God than food. You see the Word of God reveals:

* The person of God.
* The plan of God.
* The passion of God.
* The power of God.
* The principles of God.
* The perspectives of God.

Therefore if a believer does not know the Word of God, he is blind to the person, passion, power, perspective, plans and the principles of God. When we do not know His Word it becomes easy for the devil to manipulate us. When you know Him through his Word, you will discover who you are. The more you know God the more you will know the real you. Therefore you must understand that the predominant way you will know God is through and by his Word. Through his Word you will discover:

* God's plan of redemption for your spirit, soul and body.
* Your identity in and affinity with Christ.
* The plan of God for His church, Israel and the nations.
* The origin and culmination of the universe.
* Your present inheritance in Christ.
* The length, breadth and depth of the love of God for you.
* The weapons of the blood of Jesus, the name of Jesus, the armor of God, the empowerment of the Spirit as weapons to deal with the world, the flesh and the devil.

I understand God by His Word. I cannot understand God by impressions or feelings; I cannot get to know God by sentiments. If I am going to know God, I am going to know Him by His Word – Smith Wigglesworth

---

I do not read the Bible out of compulsion or religious practice. I do so with a voracious appetite of knowing my God, His character and His plan for my life. It is through knowing Him that I understand the privileges of sonship that I have. It is through knowing Him that I discover my place of dominion over the world, the flesh and the devil.

❧ Knowing God through the people over and around you

The second way you get to know God is through the people over and around you. This means through your pastors, leaders, acquaintances and friends. It is important to have the right kind of people over you and around you. Paul, in his epistle to the Corinthians, quoted the Greek Poet Menander, '*...Evil communications corrupt good manners*' (1 Corinthians 5:33). A modern rendition of this verse is, '*Bad company corrupts good character.*' Good pastors and leaders over you will give you a sense of the greatness of God. Your pastors or leaders will impart into you the power and wisdom of God. Once again, quoting the apostle Paul to the Romans, '*I long to see you that I may impart into you some spiritual gift, to the end that ye may be established*' (Romans 1:11). Your association will determine you impartation. An impartation is simply something – it could be a gift, an attribute, a mannerism, a characteristic or a trait – deposited in and communicated to you from your association with a particular person or group. That works in the positive as well as the negative. This is why it is of utmost importance who you choose to receive from or follow. Look at the positive impact Jesus had on the disciples:

> *Now when they saw the boldness of Peter and John, and perceived that they were unlearned and ignorant men, they marvelled; and they took knowledge of them, that they had been with Jesus.*
>
> ACTS 4:13

The Pharisees became aware that the association of the disciples with Jesus unleashed unbridled boldness that provoked Peter to pick up a man crippled for forty years and manifested the working of miracles at the gate called Beautiful. Now let's look at Joshua:

> *And Joshua the son of Nun was full of the spirit of wisdom; for Moses had laid his hands upon him: and the children of Israel hearkened unto him, and did as the Lord commanded Moses.*
>
> DEUTERONOMY 34:9

The association of Joshua with Moses resulted in the impartation of wisdom to lead a nation from the wilderness to the Promised land. Your leaders create the springboard for you to jump higher in life. There are people who, after spending time with them, cause you to have a sense of the greatness of God, the power of God and that you can achieve anything. On the other hand, if you hang around certain people you will have a sense of the magnitude of the devil and circumstances. Even the devil would be impressed, saying, 'I didn't know I was that big.' This is why I am careful as to who I relate to.

Your leaders create the springboard
for you to jump higher in life

My first encounter with someone who knew God with unbridled confidence was my Uncle Tony, who resides in London, England; he was responsible to lead all of our family to the Lord. I am forever grateful to him and I can never pay him for what he gave me – the Lord Jesus Christ. When you talk of raw aggressive faith, my uncle comes to my mind. He is fearless and has dominating faith. At the writing of this book he is in his seventies, strong like an ox and is still terrorizing the devil. I watched him during his immigration issue where he was challenged by the British Government and served with orders to have his whole immediate family deported from the United Kingdom. He did not panic or fall apart with depression. He went to God in prayer challenging him, 'You said in your words, every place the sole of my feet tread upon you have given to me. You also said that you created the earth. You said in your words, *the earth is the Lord's and the fulness thereof.* Now I am your child. You are in me and I am in you. Just remember this if the British Government kicks me out, they are not kicking ME out but they are kicking YOU out because you are in me.' Now that is what I called raw, unbridled, aggressive and imposing faith! At the time, as a teenager I did not understand but I saw imposing, aggressive faith (which guarantees results) in action which gave me a sense of the greatness of God. That miracle shut the mouths of all people expecting my uncle to fail. He was fearless of man and devils. I have never seen him back away from man, situation or devil. He is a hero of faith and my family love that man. Between him and my dad they exemplify imposing faith and defying impossibilities. They never take no for a final answer. If man said, 'This can't be done', they would just defy them and do it anyway. Again, as a teenager, I watched my dad being told, 'You can't buy a house because you don't make enough money.' Bank after bank refused him while other family members told him that it cannot happen but he did not care. The end result: he got the house of his dreams. These two men certainly made a direct impact upon my young mind and life.

When we were first converted, as new born believers we went to uncle Tony's cell group, where he introduced us to another great man of God by the name of Charles Sarpong (who is now with the Lord). He taught us faith, instilled in us the power of all-night prayer meetings and introduced us to R.W Schambach, Kenneth Copeland, Kenneth E Hagin, Fred Price, Benny Hinn and Jimmy Swaggart, to name a few. Being imparted by these men gave me confidence in the Word of God, the ability of God and the miraculous. I remember as a teenager how I was impacted the first time I attended a Kenneth Copeland International Believers' Convention in the late 1980's: I felt that I could go through walls and leap over walls. What happened was that I simply discovered the greatness of God and who I was in Christ Jesus. This is why you need good people over and around you; this is why you need people who know God and have had great experiences with God to speak into your life, to give you a sense of the greatness of God. Don't hang around people that magnify the devil. I am sure you have met people like that; some of them are in church! Some people, after you listen to them, cripple your faith, kill your expectation and make the devil look so big that even the devil himself is impressed. Don't give time to people like this; make time for those who know God and will boost your confidence in Him.

🐚 Knowing God through the communion of the Holy Spirit

Whenever you hear the word *communion,* your mind does not go to the Holy Spirit but to the Lord's table: the body and the blood represented by the bread and the wine. That is how we have traditionally viewed communion, and rightly so. However the Apostle Paul took communion a step further. He went beyond the Lord's table to the Lord's *tabernacle* (which is you), meaning the indwelling and habitation of the Holy Spirit within us . This was the whole purpose of Calvary: for the communion of the abiding Holy Spirit. It is through communion with Him that you will get to know God and, more directly, the specific will of God for your life or a particular situation.

You see, through the Bible, you get to know the *general* and standard plan of God for all believers – which includes you. However, through the communion of the Spirit, you get to discover the *specific* plan of God cut out for your life.

〉 What did Paul mean by communion?

I have written in depth about the communion of the Holy Spirit in my book, 'The Holy Spirit, the supernatural & you' which will be good for you to get if you want more details. The word *communion,* which in Greek is *koinonia,* was a secular word that Paul used to describe partnership, friendship, fellowship and intimacy which come from a place of sharing. These four descriptions can only be experienced through time investment and dependency upon His leadings. In other words you have to give daily increments of time to the Holy Spirit in order for you to experience His active partnership, fellowship, friendship and intimacy. The time factor that you share is how you get to know God. For you to know anyone or anything you have to invest time and communication, which are indicatives of pursuit. The law of pursuit states that you can only possess what you pursue. The effectiveness of the ministry of Jesus and Paul was their dependency upon the Holy Spirit.

It is your communion with the Holy Spirit that determines:

❖ What you carry.
❖ What you communicate.
❖ Your impartation.
❖ Your competence.

Allow me to illustrate the ministry of the Holy Spirit for your benefit from a well known story you have read in your Bible, when Jesus gave Peter a huge catch of fish. First let this verse be anchored in your mind:

Like the Spirit helpeth our infirmities...

ROMANS 8:26

The Holy Spirit is your divine helper. In fact we know the sevenfold assistance of God the Holy Spirit as our advocate, comforter, counselor, helper, intercessor, strengthener and standby power. You must ever be conscious of Him as your divine helper, meaning He will help you in any situation.

And it came to pass, that, as the people pressed upon him to hear the word of God, he stood by the lake of Gennesaret, And saw two ships standing by the lake: but the fishermen were gone out of them, and were washing their nets. And he entered into one of the ships, which was Simon's, and prayed him that he would thrust out a little from the land. And he sat down, and taught the people out of the ship. Now when he had left speaking, he said unto Simon, Launch out into the deep, and let down your nets for a draught. And Simon answering said unto him, Master, we have toiled all the night, and have taken nothing: nevertheless at thy word I will let down the net. And when they had this done, they inclosed a great multitude of fishes: and their net brake. And they beckoned unto their partners, which were in the other ship, that they should come and help them. And they came, and filled both the ships, so that they began to sink. When Simon Peter saw it, he fell down at Jesus' knees, saying,

Depart from me; for I am a sinful man, O Lord. For he was astonished, and all that were with him, at the draught of the fishes which they had taken: And so was also James, and John, the sons of Zebedee, which were partners with Simon. And Jesus said unto Simon, Fear not; from henceforth thou shalt catch men.

LUKE 5:1-10

People were pressing upon Jesus to hear the word of God. The word *pressed* in Greek is *imposed*. The people were literally imposing upon Jesus to receive a Word from heaven. He needed a platform to operate from and since He was by the sea, Jesus used the empty boat of Peter while the latter was washing his nets. This specifically means that fishing for the day was over. They had dragnet fished the night before and caught nothing except debris, which needed removal, hence the washing of the nets. Please notice the word *nets* meaning a plurality of net:

When Jesus finished teaching he declared to Peter, '*Let down your nets for a catch of fish.*'

You could hear Peter thinking to himself, '*You mean the ones which I have already washed?*'

We know he thought that by looking at how he answered Jesus, '*And Simon answering said unto him, Master, we have toiled all the night, and have taken nothing: nevertheless at thy word I will let down the net.*'

That sounded like the word of Jesus but it was not! Jesus said to throw down the *nets* but Peter said, '*I will let down the net*' meaning singular. In other words, '*I am not doing this, we have already washed the nets and put them away. Besides, last night we caught nothing. I am tired and fish do not bite in the daytime. Only an amateur would say what you said. I am professional fisherman and they did not eat last night and they certainly will not eat in the day. But just to get you off my back, I will let down a net – an old riggity and raggedy net.*'

How do we know it was an old, raggedy net? What happened when the fish came? The net broke. Now you have probably heard, '*This is what you called a net breaking, boat sinking blessing.*' The truth is a broken net and sunken boat cannot be a blessing. In order for Peter to obtain and maintain what Jesus had for him he needed the legal help of his partners. Notice these words:

> *And they beckoned unto their partners, which were in the other ship, that they should come and help them. And they came, and filled both the ships... And so was also James, and John, the sons of Zebedee, which were* **partners** *with Simon.*
>
> LUKE 5:7, 10

The word *partners* is the Greek word *koinonia*. This is a picture of the Holy Spirit. Without his partners, Peter would not have been able to capture the catch that Jesus had planned for him. It is because of his communion partnership with James and John that Peter was able to capture all that Jesus had for him. Now, your communion with the Holy Spirit will enable you to capture everything that Jesus has reserved for you. Paul shared this reality with the Corinthians, '*But as it is written, Eye hath not seen, nor ear heard, neither have entered into the heart of man,* **the things which God hath prepared for them that love him. But God hath revealed them unto us by his Spirit:** *for the Spirit searcheth all things, yea, the deep things of God.*' (1 Corinthians 2:9-10). The things that God has prepared for us! There are things prepared for you. The word *prepare* is from the Latin word *praeparare*, a combination of two words from *prae* meaning *before* and *parare* to *make ready*. This simply means before you ever came into the earth God had already prepared and made ready a lot of good stuff with your name on it. Just like when Peter saw the vision of a vessel coming down with all manner of things in it, there is a vessel with all manner of things in it just for you. However they are revealed unto you and seized by you through your communion with the Holy Spirit. A simple way of communing with the Holy Spirit is to constantly pray in tongues and consistently depend upon His leadings. By allowing yourself to be constantly led by the Spirit of God, you then develop partnership, friendship, fellowship and intimacy, taking you to the place where you know God. This intimacy with Him will lead you into accuracy and sensitivity to walk the path of His prepared plan into your prepared prosperity. There is no need to struggle. David said:

> *He maketh me to lie down in green pastures: he leadeth me beside the still waters. He restoreth my soul: he leadeth me in the paths of righteousness for his name's sake.*

PSALM 23:2-3

We will look at the exploits that are commanded through the leadings of the Holy Spirit – especially through the inward witness – in more details in the last two chapters of this book.

In order for Peter to obtain and maintain what Jesus had for him he needed the legal help of his partners. You also need the legal help of your senior partner, the mighty Holy Spirit

---

☙ Knowing God through church attendance

Don't be a smart Aleck and think you don't need church. You will get to know God by the quality of church that you attend. This is why it is incumbent upon you to find a Spirit filled and Word based church that will enhance your knowledge of God. It was through church attendance that I:

❖ Was saved.

❖ Was baptized in the Spirit with the evidence of speaking in other tongues.

❖ Learnt the Bible and the ways of God.

❖ Developed my prayer life.

❖ Satisfied my thirst for God.

❖ Increased my passion for the things of God.

❖ Discovered my purpose.

❖ Was exposed to the different giftings in the body of Christ revealing different facets of God.

The Scripture is clear that the habit of not attending church is willful sin:

Not forsaking the assembling of ourselves together, as the manner of some is; but exhorting one another: and so much the more, as ye see the day approaching. For if we sin wilfully after that we have received the knowledge of the truth, there remaineth no more sacrifice for sins,
HEBREWS 10:25-26

Don't just be a Sunday attendee only. You must be like David who penned, *'I was glad when they said unto me, Let us go into the house of the Lord'* (Psalm 122:1). Any believer who is truly dedicated to God will endeavor to be in the house of the Lord more than once a week. Think about it! The world is bombarding you 24/7 and you think going to church once weekly will make you a spiritual giant? To make matters worse, some believers have the audacity to come in late, leave early and then gripe as to why things are not working out in their lives. Then these same people who do not go to church bawl and squall when something goes wrong in their lives, saying, 'Where is God?' The reality is God is exactly where you left him. If you do not make the Word priority and the attending of church a precedence then do not blame God when things go wrong in your life. So make a plan to attend a good strong church regularly.

Don't be smart in your own eyes and think that you don't need church. Even Jesus had a habit of going to the synagogue and if He did it, so must you

---

CHAPTER 4
ONLY THE STRONG HAVE EXPLOITS

And such as do wickedly against the covenant shall he corrupt by flatteries: but the people that do know their God shall be strong, and do exploits.

DANIEL 11:32

ONLY the strong will have exploits, The weak will be exploited by the devil and circumstances. Being weak makes you subject to the ploys of the devil but being strong makes you resistant and an overcomer. As long as Abraham was weak in the flesh the devil could laugh at him in his inability to see the fulfillment of God's promise in his life. However when he became strong in faith, he laughed at the devil and saw the fulfillment of the promise in his life. We know he had the last laugh on the devil as he named the promised seed *Isaac* which means *laughter*. Faith will give you the last laugh against the devil. It requires you to be strong to overcome the wicked one.

I write unto you, fathers, because ye have known him that is from the beginning. I write unto you, young men, because ye have overcome the wicked one. I write unto you, little children, because ye have known the Father.

1 JOHN 2:13

Faith will give you the last laugh against the devil

The day everything broke

I remember when Rosanna and I first got married, things were not easy financially. I had just entered into full-time ministry and the invitations to minister were not forthcoming. Rosanna was only working part time, so money was an issue. Even though there were no invitations to minister, I would faithfully get up early, drop my wife to work and be home by 8:30am. I would then be in the Word from 9am – many times until 2pm – as well as listening or watching teaching messages. From 2pm onwards I would be in prayer. One morning I went downstairs and put the TV on and it stopped working. I thought nothing of it. Then I went to put the kettle on to make myself a hot cup of tea and the kettle broke. I thought it was one of those things that happens. Then when Rosanna came home, we went to heat some food in the microwave and that stopped working. I thought this is strange. You would have caught on earlier but I was oblivious to what was happening. She went to put some clothes in the washing machine and no sooner had she put it on that it stopped working. All of a sudden it dawned on me, 'This is an attack of the devil.'

The TV was not working nor were the kettle, microwave and washing machine. It started raining and you guessed it, the roof started to leak. To top it all, the toilet was stopped up. Even if we wanted to fix them, we could not as we had no money. I went to God in prayer: 'Lord, I have no money and all these things are broken. I need you to help me.' While in prayer, I opened my Bible and the above verse caught my attention, '*...I write unto you, young men, because ye have overcome the wicked one.*' I started to shout and rejoice in my room and kept saying, 'I am a young man and I have overcome the wicked one.' Then I stopped and listened to what I was saying. After a few seconds of pondering I spoke to the Lord, 'Lord, I know your Word says, I have written unto you young men, because you have overcome the wicked one. But right now it looks like the wicked one is overcoming me with all these things breaking down and no money.' No sooner had I said that, I heard the voice of God in my spirit, 'Well, that's what you get for reading half verses.'

I proceeded to my Bible and looked at the following verse:

I have written unto you, fathers, because ye have known him that is from the beginning. I have written unto you, young men, because ye are strong, and the word of God abideth in you, and ye have overcome the wicked one.

1 JOHN 2:14

I saw the missing link from the previous verse. Yes, I was young but in order for me to overcome the wicked one, I needed to be strong and I can only be strong when the Word is resident in me. Then and only then will I be able to overcome the wicked one. I rejoiced in that understanding. By this time it was late in the night and I fell asleep. I had a dream and saw myself standing outside of my house on the other side of the street. As I looked I saw snakes all around my property. Big snakes and little snakes. At the time I was living in London, England. There are no snakes in London. I thought to myself, 'Why are there snakes around my house?' In my dream I also saw myself with a sword in my hand and I went armed and began to cut off the heads of the snakes with my sword. I killed all the snakes with the sword in my hand then I woke up. As soon as I woke up, I knew I already had the victory. I knew the sword in the dream represented the Word of God and the snakes were demon spirits. I took authority over the devil as God showed me what to do in the dream. Then I went downstairs and miracle of miracles everything started to work. I put the TV on and it worked. The kettle worked again, as did the microwave. My uncle fixed the washing machine for nothing and somehow the roof never leaked again. For more than ten years after, the roof never leaked. It was only when we were doing a loft conversion that one of builders working on the roof said to me, 'Do you know that you have a cracked tile with a hole? Do you have leaks? I replied, 'We had a leak more than ten years ago but it has not leaked ever since.' The man shook his head in amazement and he went on to replace the tiling. This victory only became a reality because of the Word which is the sword of the Spirit. Being strong is not optional but essential.

Paul emphatically declared this sentiment to the Ephesian saints:

Finally, my brethren, be strong in the Lord, and in the power of his might.
EPHESIANS 6:10

When Paul talked about 'being strong in the Lord' he was talking about the condition and the conditioning of your spirit man because real strength is in the inner man.

That he would grant you, according to the riches of his glory, to be strengthened with might by his Spirit in the inner man
EPHESIANS 3:16

The world has a saying, 'Only the strong survive' but the Scripture makes it clear that only the strong will have exploits. To provoke unlimited exploits, you need a strong spirit. Therefore you have to look at the health and conditioning of your spirit man:

The spirit of a man will sustain his infirmity; but a wounded spirit who can bear?
PROVERBS 18:14

For as the body without the spirit is dead, so faith without works is dead also.
JAMES 2:26

Your spirit does not need your body to exist but your body needs your spirit in order to remain on the earth. We pay far too much attention to our body and neglect our spirit man. It will take strength in your inner man to resist the wiles of the devil. It will take a strong spirit to resist sicknesses and what the world is subject to. This is why you have to get your spirit man in tip-top shape. Just as a body-builder spends time to meticulously build his body, you have to meticulously build your spirit.

Let's look at the words of Solomon again:

The spirit of a man will sustain his infirmity; but a wounded spirit who can bear?

PROVERBS 18:14

A healthy spirit conquers adversity, but what can you do when the spirit is crushed?

THE MESSAGE BIBLE

The human spirit can endure in sickness, but a crushed spirit who can bear?

NEW INTERNATIONAL VERSION

The strong spirit of a man sustains him in bodily pain or trouble, but a weak and broken spirit who can raise up or bear?

AMPLIFIED BIBLE

He that hath knowledge spareth his words: and a man of understanding is of an excellent spirit.

PROVERBS 17:27 (DARBY)

He that hath knowledge spareth his words; and a man of understanding is of a cool spirit.

PROVERBS 17:27 (DARBY)

Only the strong will have exploits, The weak will be exploited by the devil and circumstances

---

The choice is yours! You can either have a strong spirit or a weak spirit. You can either be cool under pressure or be a worry wart. This is not dependent upon God, as He wants everybody strong. A strong and healthy spirit is a matter of choice and not a matter of chance.

A strong and healthy body is a matter of your choice of food and lifestyle. Eating junk food and having a lazy and immobile lifestyle will be detrimental to the health of your body. A healthy body is a well fed and well exercised body. Likewise, a healthy spirit is a well fed and well exercised spirit. As a strong and healthy body is not prone to the seasonal allergies, a strong spirit makes you immune from the elements that the devil uses. In the Bible we see different expressions for a healthy spirit:

❖ Strong spirit.
❖ Excellent spirit.
❖ Cool spirit.
❖ Merry heart/spirit.
❖ Cheerful spirit.
❖ Steadfast spirit.
❖ Faithful spirit.
❖ Humble spirit.
❖ Meek and quiet spirit.
❖ Patient spirit.

On the other hand we also see different expressions for a feeble spirit:

❖ Weak spirit.
❖ Crushed spirit.
❖ Broken spirit.
❖ Overwhelmed spirit.
❖ Troubled spirit.
❖ Vexed spirit.
❖ Hasty spirit.
❖ Proud spirit.

A strong and healthy spirit is a matter of choice
and not a matter of chance

A healthy spirit is a cool spirit that does not falter in difficult times. Some people are only cool in their clothing and looks, but fall apart cheaply when problems arise. A cool spirit is an undisturbed spirit that is not fretful in the midst of dire circumstances. Jesus, Paul and Daniel (to name a few) epitomize the reflection of a cool spirit, which does not panic. While the disciples were fretting about dying in a storm, Jesus was sleeping in the hinder part of the ship on a pillow oblivious to death and the raging wind. That's cool and strong!

Now let's look at how we can condition our spirit to be strong. We will do so by looking at how a person conditions his body to be strong in the natural. For a person to be strong and healthy, he has to:

⏻ Watch what he eats

Therefore you have to watch what you eat spiritually. Are you feeding on the meat of the Word? You cannot go to a church that dispenses doubt and unbelief – which would be spiritual junk food – and expect to be healthy. Jesus said:

> *I am the living bread which came down from heaven: if any man eat of this bread, he shall live for ever: and the bread that I will give is my flesh, which I will give for the life of the world. The Jews therefore strove among themselves, saying, How can this man give us his flesh to eat? Then Jesus said unto them, Verily, verily, I say unto you, Except ye eat the flesh of the Son of man, and drink his blood, ye have no life in you. Whoso eateth my flesh, and drinketh my blood, hath eternal life; and I will raise him up at the last day. For my flesh is meat indeed, and my blood is drink indeed. He that eateth my flesh, and drinketh my blood, dwelleth in me, and I in him.*
>
> JOHN 6:51-56

We must eat the Word of God daily through Bible reading and attending a good Word church.

---

*A cool spirit is an undisturbed spirit that is not fretful in the
midst of dire circumstances*

Walk

Just like in the natural, people who are into health do a lot of walking. We also need to walk. What should our walk be? We walk by faith and not by sight (2 Corinthians 5:7), we walk in the spirit (Galatians 5:25) and we walk in love (Ephesians 5:2). This is how we walk worthy of the Lord. Walking by faith, walking in the Spirit and the love walk will keep you free from radicals that will poison your system.

Exercise

Every healthy and strong person has an exercise routine. As we all know, exercise is good for your heart and gets rid of excess weight. Our exercise to build our spirit man is to practice the Word daily. James told us to be doers of the Word and not hearers only. The writer of Hebrews tells us, '*But strong meat belongeth to them that are of full age, even those who by reason of use have their senses exercised to discern both good and evil*' (Hebrews 5:14). Everyday you will have an opportunity to exercise yourself in the gym of God's Word. If someone criticizes you or says something demeaning, you don't have to take it personally. Exercise the Word that you know in order not to let bitterness into your heart. Do what Jesus did: 'Father, forgive them for they know not what they do.' I have had ample opportunities to be upset and lash out at people but I choose to walk the love walk. I don't take things personally. I cannot afford to have poison in my spirit. The devil might keep putting thoughts in my head but I don't let them dwell there because if I allow them to dwell in my head they will drop into my heart. Let's look at some of the exercises we must get into.

❭ Exercise to keep a clean conscience that is void of offense toward God or men.

And herein do I exercise myself, to have always a conscience void of offence toward God, and toward men.

ACTS 24:16

❭ Exercise unto godliness

But refuse profane and old wives' fables, and exercise thyself rather unto godliness.

1 TIMOTHY 4:7

❭ Exercise loving kindness

But let him that glorieth glory in this, that he understandeth and knoweth me, that I am the Lord which exercise lovingkindness, judgment, and righteousness, in the earth: for in these things I delight, saith the Lord.

JEREMIAH 9:24

I see too many believers who are quick to cut down a brother or sister. That is not loving kindness. There is an evil attitude that has crept in the church that if certain people do not agree with us then they are the enemy. I can categorically tell you that this is not godly. Your brother in Christ is not your enemy. The devil is your enemy.

❭ Exercise to have a pliable and soft heart

Delight thyself also in the Lord; and he shall give thee the desires of thine heart.

PSALM 37:4

The Hebrew word for *delight* means to be soft and pliable toward God. Exercising your heart makes it soft and pliable toward the Lord which is the antidote for hardheartedness which blocks the voice and the blessings of God.

> Exercise your prayer language

But ye, beloved, building up yourselves on your most holy faith, praying in the Holy Ghost...

JUDE 20

> Weight Training

Much have been written on the benefits of weight lifting which is also known as strength training. You can find much information online and in magazines. Let's have a quick look at some immediate benefits of strength training:

1. Speeds up your metabolism prohibiting excess weight gain. Strength training will not only make you strong, but will also help with managing your weight.
2. Improves bone density and builds muscles. In the natural as you age, the best tool that will empower you to control bone loss is to add strength training into your workout plan, which battles osteoporosis.
3. Protects the heart and fights diseases. Strength training has cardiovascular powers protecting you from heart disease. Research has revealed that strength training thrice weekly for six months reduces oxidative stress, which reduces cancer risk.
4. Increases flexibility. As you stay consistent with it, gradually, weight training improves mobility and flexibility giving you freedom of movement even as you age.

How does all this apply to you and I? The Word says that God weighs our spirit man (Proverbs 16:2). When your spirit is weighed, will you be a heavyweight or a lightweight in the Spirit? A heavyweight spirit is a trained spirit dipped in the Word and the glory of God. So we need strength training. Every time that you act the Word you are strength training. Every time that you walk in love when you've been rubbed the wrong way you are strength training your spirit man. Every time you attend a prayer meeting and fast when your flesh does not want to, that is strength training your spirit man. So, the three main things to do in order to strength train your spirit are:

❖ Act on the Word swiftly.

❖ Develop a strong prayer life.

❖ Fast often.

❭ Drink plenty of water

Every person that is into health is into water drinking. They drink lots of water daily. We have to drink of the living waters from the Lord Jesus. Drink the Word daily.

That he might sanctify and cleanse it with the washing of water by the word

EPHESIANS 5:26

And the Spirit and the bride say, Come. And let him that heareth say, Come. And let him that is athirst come. And whosoever will, let him take the water of life freely.

REVELATION 22:17

For I will pour water upon him that is thirsty, and floods upon the dry ground: I will pour my spirit upon thy seed, and my blessing upon thine offspring:

ISAIAH 44:3

❭ Take Supplements

Apart from exercising, healthy eating and drinking plenty of water, a person into health and strength will take supplements. We also need to take our supplements. Now the supplements should not replace the basics of a healthy diet, exercises and walking: you still have to maintain these things but the purpose of the supplements is to be a booster and replace what is used up in exercises and daily living. So what are our supplements?

❖ Daily listening to or watching of *faith inspiring* teachings.

Apart from my daily Bible reading, I listen to teachings everyday which has supplemented my faith and enhanced my understanding.

❖ Book reading that will supply your faith that which is lacking.

Learn to be a voracious reader. In reading you will increase in knowledge, wisdom and understanding

❖ Go to conventions and conferences

It is a great faith booster to be with like-minded people who impart passion and joy in you. Attending conventions and conferences will expose you to testimonies, revelations and new songs that will uplift your spirit.

CHAPTER 5
IMPOSING, AGGRESSIVE FAITH FOR EXPLOITS: 1

And from the days of John the Baptist until now the kingdom of heaven suffereth violence, and the violent take it by force.

MATTHEW 11:12

IT is a sad state of affairs watching most believers waiting and waiting for years to see the fulfillment of either the written promise of God's Word or a personal prophecy. It creates a cycle of frustration for the believer who does not know how to possess the land. It is one thing to know of the Promised land but there needs to a come a time in your life where you turn Promised land into Possessed land or Living land. I know you think that you sound spiritual when you say, 'I am patiently waiting on the Lord.' The truth is that Satan is robbing you of years of blessings. Many of us are waiting for things that Jesus already paid for upon the Cross of Calvary. Why should I wait and wait for years to be blessed when it already belongs to me? Wouldn't it be senseless for you to wait to drive your own car when you already paid for it? Paul already told us that all things belong to us:

Therefore let no man glory in men. For all things are yours; Whether Paul, or Apollos, or Cephas, or the world, or life, or death, or things present, or things to come; all are yours; And ye are Christ's; and Christ is God's.

1 CORINTHIANS 3:21-23

It is one thing to know of the Promised land but there needs to a come a time in your life where you turn Promised land into Possessed land

---

The reason that even though all things belong to us and yet are not ours in manifestation is because we have passive, dormant faith when we should be erupting aggressive, violent and imposing faith like Jesus said has been available, from the days of John the Baptist until now. The season changed when John the Baptist came on the scene; he was the forerunner of Jesus. When John came, he said, 'The kingdom of heaven is at hand', meaning the dominion and reign of God of heaven was ready and available to come to earth. Then Jesus came and said, 'The kingdom of God is here within you', meaning when Christ came into the earth, heaven came down to earth with the authority, power and dominion to overrule and take over. When you received Christ into your heart, heaven's dominion atmosphere was lodged in you. You don't have to wait until you die to experience heaven: you can have days of heaven upon the earth now. As you are on earth presently, you are also in heaven – seated in Christ – and since you are now already in heaven, in Jesus, then you can experience the same heavenly life now, on earth.

The nature of faith

For this to be a reality, you need Bible faith which is violent, aggressive, dominant and imposing. Faith, by nature, is an imposing force. You will hear some preachers telling you, 'Well, we are resting in Jesus.' Well that's fine! But Jesus is not your problem, it's the devil and you'd better not be resting with him. The majority of believers in Christendom are operating in passive faith and this is why we are not seeing the command of exploits on an unprecedented level. Allow me to inject an eightfold definition of imposing, aggressive faith:

1. Imposing, aggressive faith is the kind of faith that imposes itself upon Jesus, the Word, our covenant and situations.

2. Imposing, aggressive faith is the kind of faith that imposes itself upon God, Jesus, the Word and our covenant to possess the promises of God and Zoe: God kind of life.

3. Imposing, aggressive faith is the kind of faith that does not take *no* as a final answer.

4. Imposing, aggressive faith is the kind of faith that bullies the devil, demons and situations.

5. Imposing, aggressive faith is the kind of faith that takes and not waits.

6. Imposing, aggressive faith is the kind of faith that puts its weight on a situation.

7. Imposing, aggressive faith is the kind of faith that dominates, overcomes and is not undermined.

8. Imposing, aggressive faith is the kind of faith that causes Jesus to stop and follow you to your house.

Meditate upon these eightfold definitions until they sink deep into your spirit. I want you to get this in your mind and spirit: imposing, aggressive faith is the kind of faith that will oppose and bully the devil. No longer will the devil bully you and exploit you! It is the kind of faith that will intimidate devils, like Jesus did when He walked into a room and His faith filled the atmosphere. Imposing, aggressive faith is the kind of faith that presses on Jesus, His Word, the Holy Spirit and the covenant for the manifestation of miracles. Jairus displayed it; the woman with the issue of blood had it; Bartimaeus had it; the centurion exemplified it; Jesus walked in it; Paul lived it; Jephthah thrived on it. Imposing, aggressive faith will never take no as a final answer. It cannot take no as a final answer because of what Paul said:

For all the promises of God in him are yea, and in him Amen, unto the glory of God by us.

2 CORINTHIANS 1:20

For no matter how many promises God has made, they are "Yes" in Christ. And so through him the "Amen" is spoken by us to the glory of God.

NEW INTERNATIONAL VERSION

For as many as are the promises of God, they all find their Yes [answer] in Him [Christ]. For this reason we also utter the Amen (so be it) to God through Him [in His Person and by His agency] to the glory of God.
                                                                AMPLIFIED BIBLE

Never settle for *no* when God has said *yes*. The reason we settle for no is because many believers possess passive faith. As I just mentioned, faith is imposing, aggressive and forward-moving in nature. It is through this kind of faith that everything becomes a reality. Without faith we could not even access the grace of God that procured redemption.

Imposing aggressive faith is the kind of faith that will oppose and bully the devil. It is the kind of faith that will intimidate the devil

---

*Therefore **it is of faith, that it might be by grace**; to the end the promise might be sure to all the seed; not to that only which is of the law, but to that also which is of the faith of Abraham; who is the father of us all*
                                                                ROMANS 4:16

For by grace are ye saved through faith; and that not of yourselves: it is the gift of God:
                                                                EPHESIANS 2:8

Grace without faith is frustrating. Do you know that we can frustrate the grace of God? Look at the words of the Apostle Paul to the Galatians, '*I do not frustrate the grace of God: for if righteousness come by the law, then Christ is dead in vain.*' (Galatians 2:21). There are millions of believers frustrating God today. Frustrate (from the Latin word *frustrat*) means *disappointed*, which is derived from the verb frustrare and from frustra meaning *in vain*. Therefore when Paul said that we can frustrate the grace of God, it is as if the grace was never shed, although it has already been shed. How do we frustrate the grace of God? How do we frustrate and render His grace in vain? The answer is found in the verse, '...*for if righteousness comes by the law, then Christ is dead in vain.*' How does righteousness and salvation come? By grace through faith (Ephesians 2:8). We frustrate the grace of God when there is no faith to draw upon what He has made available. Grace is frustrated when there is no imposing, aggressive faith to draw on its favors. It looks as if grace never made provision when that is not the case. It takes faith to access the grace of God. Just saying to people that nothing needs to be done because Jesus has done everything is partly true, but the whole is it takes faith to appropriate all the benefits and favors that grace gives. Grace is what He is and has accomplished whereas faith is what I employ to seize with a clear conscience what Jesus paid for on the Cross. Grace without faith is like an inheritance without an estate attorney: just as an estate attorney makes sure that the beneficiary receives what is prepared or left for him, your faith will ensure that you receive what grace made available to you.

Grace is frustrated when there is no imposing,
aggressive faith to draw on its favors

Real Bible faith is aggressive, imposing itself upon a situation and even upon God. Jesus said it this way, '*And from the days of John the Baptist until now the kingdom of heaven suffereth violence, and the violent take it by force*' (Matthew 11:12). The Bengel's Gnomon Commentary of the New Testament explains this verse as, '*βιάζεται, pushes itself forward as it were by violence. Consider attentively ch. Matthew 13:32-33, and Luke 14:23. The LXX. frequently use βιάζομαι, to signify, to employ force.*'

The above commentary says *kingdom faith* pushes itself forward by force and is imposing. Anyone that ever received a miracle in the ministry of Jesus did so by imposing their faith upon him. Let's look at a few examples in the Scriptures.

1 Jairus

And when Jesus was passed over again by ship unto the other side, much people gathered unto him: and he was nigh unto the sea. And, behold, there cometh one of the rulers of the synagogue, Jairus by name; and when he saw him, he fell at his feet, And besought him greatly, saying, My little daughter lieth at the point of death: I pray thee, come and lay thy hands on her, that she may be healed; and she shall live. And Jesus went with him; and much people followed him, and thronged him.

MARK 5:21-24

This is a clear example of imposing, aggressive faith. When Jesus recrossed to the other side of the lake there was a huge crowd of people waiting on Him. Obviously the crowd had gathered because they all needed a miracle. If they had no need there would be no need for them to gather. So all those who were gathered were there for the purpose of catching the attention of Jesus in order for them to get their respective miracle. It was not a little crowd; many of the modern translations state that it was a large or vast crowd. This is an important point to grasp. It was not a handful of people but a large crowd. When Jesus disembarked from the boat, something uncommon happened:

*The leader of the local synagogue, whose name was Jairus, came and fell down before him, pleading with him to heal his little daughter. She is at the point of death, he said in desperation. Please come and place your hands on her and make her live. **Jesus went with him, and the crowd thronged behind.**'*

LIVING BIBLE

Out of the whole, large crowd that came looking for a miracle, Jesus went to the house of Jairus. Can you hear the murmurings of some in the crowd? 'That's not fair, I have been waiting here for a long time.' Hear the murmuring of another, 'I was here first. The audacity of that man to jump the line. Who does he think he is?'

What is amazing is that Jesus never questioned who had been waiting for the longest but just followed Jairus. Now you can hear the collective murmuring, 'That's just not fair!' No, it is not fair, it is faith – Imposing, aggressive faith to be more precise.

Imposing, aggressive faith is the kind of faith that imposes itself upon Jesus, the Word, our covenant and situations

---

What is even more interesting is that Jesus left the crowd and followed Jairus. For years we have been taught, 'Faith is following Jesus' but what Jairus is teaching us is 'Faith is to get Jesus to follow you.' Did you catch that? Faith is more than you following Jesus but to get Jesus to follow you. Now He will not follow fear, doubt or unbelief. But if you have any ounce of faith and confidence, He is coming to your house. See the picture now: Jairus is leading the way, Jesus is following and the crowd are following them. Now you know the crowd did not want to go to Jairus' house. They would have preferred for Jesus to come to their house. Why did He not? Because they were passive and Jairus operated with imposing, aggressive faith. Imposing, aggressive faith will get Jesus to your house. How can we know that Jairus was operating in imposing, aggressive faith?

*And, behold, there cometh one of the rulers of the synagogue, Jairus by name; and when he saw him, he fell at his feet, And **besought** him greatly, saying, My little daughter lieth at the point of death: I pray thee, come and lay thy hands on her, that she may be healed; and she shall live.*

MARK 5:22-23

The word *besought* is the key to this verse. When you read that it gives you an image of begging because that is how we define the word *besought*. However in Greek it is the word *parakaleo,* meaning to call to one side and to summon. While everyone there had a passive, begging mentality, Jairus was the one who broke out of the crowd and imposed himself upon Jesus. Jairus figured within himself that a drastic situation demands drastic action.

He imposed his faith upon the crowd, the sickness and upon Jesus. Notice that Jesus did not argue with him but followed him to his house. By the way, Jairus operated in imposing, aggressive faith because his very name 'Jairus' means 'enlightened by the Word'. When you have the light of the Word in you then you will manifest imposing, aggressive faith.

2 Woman with the issue of blood

While Jesus is following Jairus and the crowd are following them, there is another turn of events with a woman who imposed her faith on the procession to Jairus' house:

> *And a certain woman, which had an issue of blood twelve years, And had suffered many things of many physicians, and had spent all that she had, and was nothing bettered, but rather grew worse, When she had heard of Jesus, came in the press behind, and touched his garment. For she said, If I may touch but his clothes, I shall be whole. And straightway the fountain of her blood was dried up; and she felt in her body that she was healed of that plague. And Jesus, immediately knowing in himself that virtue had gone out of him, turned him about in the press, and said, Who touched my clothes?*
>
> MARK 5:25-30

What we read here can be best described as a miracle within a miracle. I also want to remind you of Dr Luke's account of the same event. Of course Luke is recounting this event from a medical perspective where he said, '*And a woman having an issue of blood twelve years, which had spent all her living upon physicians, neither could be healed of any*' (Luke 8:43). In other words, it was beyond Medical Science's ability to bring relief and a cure to this woman. Beside the physical aspect, according to the Levitical Law, '*the disease from which this woman suffered made her ceremonially unclean separating her in a great measure for a very long period from all contact with the outer world*' (Pulpit Commentary).

There were seven things against this woman. She was:

❖ Ceremonially unclean.

❖ Socially unacceptable.

❖ Physically depleted.

❖ Financially broke.

❖ In an obstructing, large crowd.

❖ With Jairus, the ruler of the synagogue, who can legally demand that she be stoned to death.

All the odds were against her and yet by imposing, aggressive faith she obtained a great miracle. Her imposing faith caused the procession to stop and for Jesus to ask, 'Who touched my clothes, for I perceive that virtue has left me' (Luke 8:46). When she came forward to testify, Jesus told her, 'Your faith has made you whole.'

That's the imposing, aggressive God kind of faith that will stop a procession!

The imposing, aggressive kind of faith that defies all odds and fears to obtain what it wants!

The imposing, violent kind of faith that will push through an obstructing crowd from behind to get to the front.

That's real Bible faith in action.

From the crowd that came to see and follow Jesus, only the two that imposed their faith were the ones who received their miracles. While others observed, these two obtained.

Passive faith observes; imposing, aggressive faith obtains

---

3 Bartimaeus

And they came to Jericho: and as he went out of Jericho with his disciples and a great number of people, blind Bartimæus, the son of Timæus, sat by the highway side begging. And when he heard that it was Jesus of Nazareth, he began to cry out, and say, Jesus, thou Son of David, have mercy on me. And many charged him that he should hold his peace: but he cried the more a great deal, Thou Son of David, have mercy on me. And Jesus stood still, and commanded him to be called. And they call the blind man, saying unto him, Be of good comfort, rise; he calleth thee. And he, casting away his garment, rose, and came to Jesus. And Jesus answered and said unto him, What wilt thou that I should do unto thee? The blind man said unto him, Lord, that I might receive my sight.

MARK 10:46-51

Once again, notice there was a crowd that was following Jesus but only Bartimaeus was aggressive and imposed himself upon Jesus to obtain his sight. As soon as Baritmaeus heard that Jesus of Nazareth was walking by, although he was sitting by as a beggar, he decided his begging days were over. Many were vying for the attention and touch of Jesus but only he got it because he engaged imposing, aggressive faith. The crowd endeavored to shut him down but that did not curtail his demand upon Jesus because he got even louder and what was the end result? '*And Jesus stood still and commanded him to be called.*' I like how The Message translation pens this verse, '*Jesus stopped in his tracks. Call him over.*' Out of the multitude only Bartimaeus dared to impose on Jesus and stop Him in His tracks. Notice how imposing, aggressive faith broke the stronghold of begging, waiting and the naysayers. Imposing, aggressive faith is not the faith that waits but the faith that takes. It is not the kind of faith that says, 'one day it will happen' but says, 'It's happening today.' Imposing, aggressive faith is not squelched by people's disapproval. Imposing, aggressive faith will never allow the devil and the voice of circumstances to shout you down. Imposing, aggressive faith does not get shouted down but shouts down all the negative voices.

---

*Imposing aggressive faith is not squelched
by people's disapproval*

---

4 Four crazy friends

And again he entered into Capernaum after some days; and it was noised that he was in the house. And straightway many were gathered together, insomuch that there was no room to receive them, no, not so much as about the door: and he preached the word unto them. And they come unto him, bringing one sick of the palsy, which was borne of four. And when they could not come nigh unto him for the press, they uncovered the roof where he was: and when they had broken it up, they let down the bed wherein the sick of the palsy lay. When Jesus saw their faith, he said unto the sick of the palsy, Son, thy sins be forgiven thee.

MARK 2:1-5

Here's another example of imposing, aggressive faith in action in the form of four friends who were determined to get a miracle for their friend. Dr Luke's account reveals an interesting point:

And, behold, men brought in a bed a man which was taken with a palsy: **and they sought means to bring him in, and to lay him before him. And when they could not find by what way they might bring him in because of the multitude,** *they went upon the housetop...*

LUKE 5:18-19

These four friends could not find a way to bring the afflicted one before Jesus who was in the house because of the huge crowd. In other words when they came to the front door, it was jammed with people. They went to the back door and they faced the same scene: people blocking their entrance. They would have gone to the window only to find there were also people there vying for the touch of the Great Physician. Did that deter these four men? Not one bit. What they did next demonstrated the act of imposing, aggressive faith. They went on top of the house of Jesus[1] and tore the roof off. You cannot get anymore imposing and audacious than that.

---

1   Also Mark 2:1-4. Some scholars believe this was Jesus' own house.

If that was your house and you saw someone tear off your roof you would be saying, in no uncertain terms, 'You'd better pay to fix that roof!' Look at the reaction of Jesus: *'When Jesus saw their faith...'* He was not mad with them, but He saw something in them. What did He see? He saw their imposing, aggressive faith that didn't think twice about tearing the roof off but did so with shameless confidence, clearing the way for their friend to be in the middle of the house for a healing.

You see, imposing, aggressive faith is shameless in its actions with the view of getting before Jesus. It will go over and above the rest of the crowd to the place of no denial. Imposing and dominant faith becomes the center of attraction in a situation through shameless confidence and an unrelenting push for the hand of God; it makes a spectacle of itself, not for the attention of people or just to create a scene but to shake the devil off and command the attention of God.

Faith by nature is an imposing, aggressive force that will not take no as a final answer

---

5 Jesus

If there was ever a person who epitomized raw, imposing, aggressive and dominant faith, it was Jesus. He would take over a situation. Going back to the event of Jairus' daughter where Jesus was following him to his house, we know that in the middle of the procession, the woman with the issue of blood interrupted them to get her miracle and later came forward to testify. During that period bad news came:

> *While he yet spake, there came from the ruler of the synagogue's house certain which said, **Thy daughter is dead: why troublest thou the Master any further?** As soon as Jesus heard the word that was spoken, he saith unto the ruler of the synagogue, Be not afraid, only believe.*
>
> MARK 5:35-36

As soon as Jesus heard the bad report that came from Jairus' house, He attacked unbelief and death; He shot back at the words of death. Observe that from that point on you never hear about Jairus again? It is all about Jesus and how He dominated, taking over the wake or the vigil, kicking out those who were weeping and mocking in unbelief.

> *And he cometh to the house of the ruler of the synagogue, and seeth the tumult, and them that wept and wailed greatly. And when he was come in, he saith unto them, Why make ye this ado, and weep? the damsel is not dead, but sleepeth. And they laughed him to scorn. But when he had put them all out, he taketh the father and the mother of the damsel, and them that were with him, and entereth in where the damsel was lying. And he took the damsel by the hand, and said unto her, Talitha cumi; which is, being interpreted, Damsel, I say unto thee, arise. And straightway the damsel arose, and walked; for she was of the age of twelve years. And they were astonished with a great astonishment.*
>
> MARK 5:38-42

Imposing and dominant faith puts you in a place of command. Notice they laughed at Jesus, but He had the last laugh. When you operate in imposing, aggressive faith be aware people will not understand and they will mock and disdain you. That's OK! Because you will have the last word and the last laugh. If you don't impose your faith, they will impose their unbelief. While Jesus was on His way following the imposing Jairus, one came from his house with this testimony, 'Thy daughter is dead: why troublest thou the Master any further?' (Mark 5:35). If you do not impose your faith, the devil will impose defeat. When Jesus arrived at the house of Jairus, they laughed him to scorn when He said the girl was not dead. Instead of allowing them to impose their unbelief upon Him, He imposed His faith upon them by kicking them out.

If you do not impose faith, the enemy will impose fear. Jesus imposed His faith at Lazarus' grave, at Jairus' house and when He was in the boat during the storm. He was not the victim of exterior forces but made exterior negative forces be subject to Him. Whether it was weather, demons, death, sicknesses or funeral, Jesus took over and imposed His faith to obtain the desired results.

If you don't impose your faith, they will impose their unbelief

---

CHAPTER 6
IMPOSING, AGGRESSIVE FAITH FOR EXPLOITS: 2

WE are continuing on our train of thought of imposing and aggressive faith for exploits by looking at the life of Jesus and others. All who received their miracles were those who exerted imposing and dominant faith on Jesus. If you want to do great exploits this year then you need to walk in the same kind of faith.

6 Mary the mother of Jesus

And the third day there was a marriage in Cana of Galilee; and the mother of Jesus was there: And both Jesus was called, and his disciples, to the marriage. And when they wanted wine, the mother of Jesus saith unto him, They have no wine. Jesus saith unto her, Woman, what have I to do with thee? mine hour is not yet come. His mother saith unto the servants, Whatsoever he saith unto you, do it.

JOHN 2:1-5

Through this miracle of turning water into wine, we see the imposing faith of Mary. Jesus and His disciples attended the wedding as well as Mary. During the celebration the wedding party ran out of wine, which would have been a social embarrassment in that culture – or any culture for that matter. It would not have been a matter for concern if they had the money to just go and buy more. The fact that it became a concern indicates there was no money left. No money, no more wine but plenty of guests at the wedding. Mary jumped to the occasion and took charge. She came to Jesus and told Him bluntly, 'They have no wine' with the mindset that He had to do something. Although Jesus told her that His time of manifestation was not due, that did not deter Mary one bit who further imposed herself on the servants saying, 'Whatever He tells you to do, do it.' The rest of the story is a great miracle but it could not have happened if Mary did not exert imposing and dominant faith.

7 Syrophoenician woman

Then Jesus went thence, and departed into the coasts of Tyre and Sidon. And, behold, a woman of Canaan came out of the same coasts, and cried unto him, saying, Have mercy on me, O Lord, thou Son of David; my daughter is grievously vexed with a devil. But he answered her not a word. And his disciples came and besought him, saying, Send her away; for she crieth after us. But he answered and said, I am not sent but unto the lost sheep of the house of Israel. Then came she and worshipped him, saying, Lord, help me. But he answered and said, It is not meet to take the children's bread, and to cast it to dogs. And she said, Truth, Lord: yet the dogs eat of the crumbs which fall from their masters' table. Then Jesus answered and said unto her, O woman, great is thy faith: be it unto thee even as thou wilt. And her daughter was made whole from that very hour.

MATTHEW 15:21-28

When we talk about imposing and aggressive faith this woman is a perfect candidate. The Scriptures make it clear that she was a Canaanite; Mark, in his Gospel, described her as Greek-Syrophoenician meaning that she was outside the commonwealth of Israel and out of dispensation. She was a Gentile and Gentiles were pictured as dogs in Jewish mentality because of being non-covenant people. When she came to Jesus with her request, at first Jesus did not even acknowledge or answer her. If that happened today, people would have been offended at Jesus, but not this woman. She kept pestering and would not take no as an answer and focused her attention between Jesus and the disciples to the point where they were flabbergasted and asked Jesus to get rid of her. She would not be denied and took it a step further and worshiped Jesus saying, 'Lord, help me'. Jesus' reply to her was not complimentary, *'It is not meet to take the children's bread, and to cast it to dogs'* but her answer was exemplary, *'Truth, Lord: yet the dogs eat of the crumbs which fall from their masters' table.'*

Faith is doing what He tells you to do
without arguing or fretting

That was the *faith imposing response* that provoked Jesus to do a mighty exploit for this out of dispensation, out of time, out of covenant Gentile woman. Jesus said she had great faith. In Greek the word great is *mega*. Therefore imposing and dominant faith is mega faith that will not allow itself to be denied. The doctor may have told you that you are out of time and given up on you but your faith will not give up on you. Like Abraham, the aggressiveness of imposing faith will cause you to hope against natural hope and defy all oppositions to win.

8 The Centurion

And when Jesus was entered into Capernaum, there came unto him a centurion, beseeching him, And saying, Lord, my servant lieth at home sick of the palsy, grievously tormented. And Jesus saith unto him, I will come and heal him. The centurion answered and said, Lord, I am not worthy that thou shouldest come under my roof: but speak the word only, and my servant shall be healed. For I am a man under authority, having soldiers under me: and I say to this man, Go, and he goeth; and to another, Come, and he cometh; and to my servant, Do this, and he doeth it. When Jesus heard it, he marvelled, and said to them that followed, Verily I say unto you, I have not found so great faith, no, not in Israel.
MATTHEW 8:5-10

Here is another example of a man who is not part of the covenant but who made a demand upon Jesus to come to his house to heal his servant who was dear to him and was at the point of death. Luke, in his account said the servant was ready to die (Luke 7:2). Here is a Gentile who through imposing and dominant faith manages to convince a Jew to go into the house of a Gentile. While Jesus is on the way, Luke records, *'Then Jesus went with them. **And when he was now not far from the house, the centurion sent friends to him**, saying unto him, Lord, trouble not thyself: for I am not worthy that thou shouldest enter under my roof: **Wherefore neither thought I myself worthy to come unto thee:** but say in a word, and my servant shall be healed. For I also am a man set under authority, having under me soldiers, and I say unto one, Go, and he goeth; and to another, Come, and he cometh; and to my servant, Do this, and he doeth it'* (Luke 7:6-8).

Imposing and dominant faith is mega faith that will not allowed itself to be denied

---

The gall of this man. He did not even go to see Jesus himself but sent friends to tell Jesus there was no need for him to come to the house. We know that Jesus was already near the house but the Centurion went even further in dominant faith by drawing from his military experience in commanding things to be executed simply by his commands. Jesus did not argue and say, 'Well I am already near the house, so I might as well come in and get it done.' No that did not happen! If that was you, you would probably have been offended? You would rationalize in your head, 'First he does not come to me himself but sends people to ask for a request. Secondly he gets me to leave where I am, to come to his place. Thirdly while I am near his house he decides it is not important for me to come into his house. Fourthly he does not even have the respect to come and tell me that himself. Fifthly he has the audacity to tell me to speak a word. You know what, does he know who I am? I am offended that he would treat me like this. He can go fly a kite and leave me alone.'

That was not how Jesus reacted. The Lord was impressed with this man's imposing and audacious faith:

> *When Jesus heard it, he marvelled, and said to them that followed, Verily I say unto you, I have not found **so great faith, no, not in Israel**. And I say unto you, That many shall come from the east and west, and shall sit down with Abraham, and Isaac, and Jacob, in the kingdom of heaven. But the children of the kingdom shall be cast out into outer darkness: there shall be weeping and gnashing of teeth.*
>
> MATTHEW 8:10-12

This is the second person that Jesus said had mega imposing faith and he was a Gentile. Think about what this Centurion did to Jesus. He mobilized Jesus to come to his house without being personally asking Him. He then stopped Jesus from walking into his house and still got his miracle. He was dictating the steps of Jesus. This is aggressive, imposing and dominant faith.

It is time for you to rise with imposing faith, the kind of faith that takes, not with the faith that waits. It is time for you to receive what Jesus already paid for. The man who was crippled from birth and sat at the gate called Beautiful exemplifies the right attitude that you must have:

> *And he gave heed unto them, expecting to receive something of them.*
>
> ACTS 3:5

The word receive is *lambano* in Greek meaning to seize, to take, to lay hold of aggressively. It is time for you to lambano your breakthroughs, your miracles and your healing. Why wait when you can take? The day that you decide that your waiting days are over you will start living in the now and experience blessings in the now.

Why wait when you can take?

---

9   The man who was sick for 38 years

Now there is at Jerusalem by the sheep market a pool, which is called in the Hebrew tongue Bethesda, having five porches. In these lay a great multitude of impotent folk, of blind, halt, withered, waiting for the moving of the water. For an angel went down at a certain season into the pool, and troubled the water: whosoever then first after the troubling of the water stepped in was made whole of whatsoever disease he had. And a certain man was there, which had an infirmity thirty and eight years. When Jesus saw him lie, and knew that he had been now a long time in that case, he saith unto him, Wilt thou be made whole? The impotent man answered him, Sir, I have no man, when the water is troubled, to put me into the pool: but while I am coming, another steppeth down before me. Jesus saith unto him, Rise, take up thy bed, and walk. And immediately the man was made whole, and took up his bed, and walked: and on the same day was the sabbath.

JOHN 5:1-9

☙ Passive and Aggressive Faith

This event of the miracle which occurred for the man who had been sick for 38 years is a contrast between passive faith and imposing, aggressive faith. Take note: the pool was by the sheep market. Anyone with Bible sense will know that sheep represent the children of God. Secondly the pool was called Bethesda which means the 'house of mercy', suggesting mercy flows for the child of God to be healed and delivered. This is a picture of grace and faith. The pool is representative of grace that flows and the man at the sheep gate is a type of aggressive, imposing faith to obtain mercy and find grace to help in time of need (Hebrews 4:16). He moved from passive faith into aggressive faith that brought to an end his 38 years of affliction. As long as the man operated in passive faith, he remained afflicted and others would step ahead of him to get the miracle. So many believers are operating in passive faith.

---

*Imposing, aggressive faith becomes the center of attraction
in a situation through shameless confidence and an
unrelenting push for the hand of God*

☙ What do I mean by passive faith?

The Oxford English dictionary defines passive as 'accepting or allowing what happens or what others do, without active response or resistance.' This is where many believers are, with no resistance to the devil and circumstances while still believing in God and going to church. Notice the dictionary defines it as *accepting and allowing what happens or what someone else does without active resistance.* If you allow it and accept it then you cannot blame God and ask, 'Where is God in all this?'

God already gave you His Word, His armor, the Holy Spirit, the blood of Jesus and the name of Jesus to stop the devil. What more do you need? It is up to you to put a stop to the enemy. If you are not resisting the devil then you are assisting him. In His Word, God has said:

Resist the devil, and he will flee from you.

JAMES 4:7

Above all, taking the shield of faith, wherewith ye shall be able to quench all the fiery darts of the wicked.

EPHESIANS 6:16

The man's problem was that he was willing to wait and wait and wait without ever appropriating. He was looking for a man to help him into the water. Why would anyone help him to get in the water when they were there themselves looking to be healed? Whoever jumped in first was made whole of whatsoever disease they had – without exception. That was a sweet deal that could be tasted by the one who was aggressive enough to jump before everyone else. Jesus shoved that man from a state of passivity and waiting on the hand of others to help him get what he wanted, to a place of aggressive faith to take what he came for. He took his healing and he took his bed home simply by tapping into aggressive faith.

Your exploits will materialize when you engage imposing, aggressive faith. Stop waiting for somebody in America or Europe to help you. God is your helper and He is not American, European or African. Your faith is what will help you. Stop saying, 'If I lived in a different country things would be better.' No! Things can be better *now* with faith.

If you are not resisting the devil then you are assisting him

---

CHAPTER 7
TEN EXPLOITS OF FAITH

IT is your birthright to experience unlimited exploits in your life, finances, family, career, ministry and whatever field that you're in. Abraham's exploits of faith were spiritual, financial and physical. His faith reversed the impotence of a ninety-nine year old body and the wheels of nature to father a child. You can find the celebrated exploits of the main patriarchs throughout the Old Testament and of course in the eleventh chapter of Hebrews. I specifically want to focus on four verses to give you ten exploits of imposing faith.

> *And what shall I more say? for the time would fail me to tell of Gedeon, and of Barak, and of Samson, and of Jephthae; of David also, and Samuel, and of the prophets: Who through faith subdued kingdoms, wrought righteousness, obtained promises, stopped the mouths of lions, Quenched the violence of fire, escaped the edge of the sword, out of weakness were made strong, waxed valiant in fight, turned to flight the armies of the aliens. Women received their dead raised to life again: and others were tortured, not accepting deliverance; that they might obtain a better resurrection:*
>
> HEBREWS 11:32-35

1 FAITH THAT PROVOKES EXPLOITS SUBDUES KINGDOMS

Jesus said, '*And from the days of John the Baptist until now the kingdom of heaven suffereth violence, and the violent take it by force.*' (Matthew 11:12). In other words the kingdom of God is forcefully advancing taking territories from the kingdom of darkness. In order for the kingdom of God to forcefully advance, it has to subdue the kingdom of darkness. To subdue means to pressure it beneath you. Abraham and Sarah subdued nature. David subdued the giant Goliath. You will subdue the kingdom of darkness in your vicinity. The word *violent* in Greek is *beeastace* meaning an enforcer and one who crowds or imposes himself upon a situation. Faith is an enforcer and imposer of the rule of heaven upon the earth. This verse can be literally translated as:

'From the days of John the Baptist until now, the rule of heaven is enforced or imposed upon the reign of death and the imposer takes it by raw power.'

Your faith is the imposer of the rule of heaven on the earth. That's what I call imposing, aggressive, violent faith. We will deal with this in a later chapter. This is not the kind of faith that waits but the faith that takes.

2 FAITH THAT PROVOKES EXPLOITS RULES WELL AND ENFORCES JUSTICE

Our Authorized Version says, 'wrought righteousness' but modern translations say, 'rule well or enforce justice'. Violent faith will equip to rule well over the affairs of life. Like the widow in the parable of the unjust judge, justice will have to be done on your behalf.

3 FAITH THAT PROVOKES EXPLOITS OBTAINS PROMISES

There needs to come a time in your life when promised land becomes living land. For too many believers there is a discrepancy between what they read in the Scriptures and what they experience in life. They see the promised land in the Scriptures but they live in the problem land in life. Like David, Joshua and Caleb you will also obtain promises.

4 FAITH THAT PROVOKES EXPLOITS STOPS THE MOUTHS OF LIONS

Peter revealed that our adversary, the devil is as a roaring lion seeking whom he may devour. Now he cannot devour everybody and anybody. He is looking for easy prey. The word '*adversary*' in Greek is *antidikos* which is a combination of two words, *anti* meaning against or to deny and *dikos* meaning rights. So when you combine the two words together it means one who denies you your rights. Satan will no longer deny you your rights and devour you. Like Daniel you will not be devoured by the mouths of lions.

5 FAITH THAT PROVOKES EXPLOITS QUENCHES THE VIOLENCE OF FIRE

Paul told the Ephesian saints, *'Above all taking up the shield of faith, wherewith you shall be able to quench all the fiery darts of the wicked one'* (Ephesians 6:16). Whatever fire is raging against you will be quenched like the fire which had no power of Shadrach, Meshach and Abed-Nego although it was turned up seven times hotter. These three Hebrew boys were walking freer in the fire than they were before they were thrown in the fiery furnace. We have a promise from the book, *'when thou walkest through the fire, thou shalt not be burned; neither shall the flame kindle upon thee'* (Isaiah 43:2). As you lift up the shield of faith – which in Greek is the word *thureos* from *thura*, meaning *as big as a door* – your faith will cover you from the top of your head to the tip of your toes and shield you from fiery darts of the wicked one by the water of the Word on it.

6 FAITH THAT PROVOKES EXPLOITS ESCAPES THE EDGE OF THE SWORD

The edge of the sword speaks of death and an execution. Whatever death sentence has been pronounced over your life from the curse of a witchdoctor, the spell of a hater, infirmity in your lineage or the sentence of a doctor can be revoked by the double edged sword of the Word of God. Peter escaped the edge of the sword of Herod as the church engaged importunate praying in faith. Don't sit there and cry over words which have been spoken over your life, wringing your hands like you don't know what to do. Let the Word of the Almighty be a double edged sword in your mouth, decreeing your victory over the works of the devil. Why do you think God gave you His Word? It was not for mental gymnastics but to use it as a weapon and a way of escape from every plot of the prince of darkness.

7 Faith that provokes exploits turns weakness into strength

Abraham and Sarah turned their weakness into strength. Aggressive faith will always trigger a turning point in your life. As Paul himself declared when he was writing from prison to the Philippian saints:

> *For I know that this shall turn to my salvation through your prayer, and the supply of the Spirit of Jesus Christ, According to my earnest expectation and my hope, that in nothing I shall be ashamed...*
>
> Philippians 1:19-20

He expected things to turn in his favor and deliverance even though he was in jail. He did not anticipate the worst but the best. It was according to his expectation and the Scriptures tells us clearly, *'For surely there is an end; and thine expectation shall not be cut off'* (Proverbs 23:18). Fear not! You can also turn things for the better around you.

8 Faith that provokes exploits waxes valiant in fight

You will not get weaker but stronger and better. On the island of Melita, after being bitten by a snake, the islanders came to the conclusion that this was judgment on Paul and were waiting to see him convulse and drop dead. However, the more they watched, the more he stood and they had to change their minds about him. This is exactly what will happen to you. There are people and devils waiting for you to drop dead but you will disappoint them. Like the mighty men of David, you will do well in battle.

Like Josheb-basshebeth the Tachmonite, who wielded his spear in battle against eight hundred men and killed them at one time. He did not have a machine gun or semi automatic yet he got them all. He was the original Rambo or Terminator (2 Samuel 23:8).

Like Eleazar the son of Dodo the Ahohite, who defied the Philistines that came to battle, and the men of Israel had deserted him. He fought and killed the Philistines. Although he was exhausted and his hand got tired but his hand cleaved to his sword and the Lord gave him a great victory that day. The people who deserted him later returned after he won the battle for the spoil. In battle you will not lose your sword but you will cleave to it until you win (2 Samuel 23:9-10).

Like Shammah who, when the Philistines were gathered together into a troop, where there was a piece of ground full of lentiles: and once again the people fled from the Philistines. But he stood in the midst of the ground, and defended it, and slew the Philistines with God giving him a great victory (2 Samuel 23:11-12).

Like Benaiah the son of Jehoida, the son of a valiant man, of Kabzeel, who had great exploits slaying two lionlike men of Moab. One time Benaiah went down and killed a lion in a pit in time of snow. You will also beat the devil on his own turf. One time Benaiah was fighting an Egyptian who had a spear in his hand and he went down to him with a staff, and snatched the spear out of the Egyptian's hand, and killed him with his own spear (2 Samuel 23:20-21).

There are people and devils waiting for you to drop dead but you will disappoint them

---

9 FAITH TURNS TO FLIGHT THE ARMY OF ALIENS

Like the Philistines ran from David after he killed their champion Goliath, you will also cause those who come against you one way to flee seven ways. A thousand will fall at your side and ten thousand at your right hand but they will not come near you (Psalm 91:7).

10 FAITH THAT PROVOKES EXPLOITS RECEIVES THE DEAD RAISED TO LIFE

The widow of Zarephath had her son back from the dead when she engaged the prophetic ministry of Elijah. The Shunammite woman received her son back from the dead when she engaged the ministry of Elisha. The widow of Nain had her son raised from the dead when she encountered the ministry of Jesus. These women had aggressive faith and would not take death as the final word over their son's lives. Death did not have the last word over Jesus' life. So don't let any dead issue bury you before your time.

〉 Don't make excuses for lack of exploits

You will always find somebody who will give you an excuse why they cannot have exploits. In fact they will use the Bible to justify their fruitless lives. Some will even use Hebrews 11 as an excuse:

> *...and others were tortured, not accepting deliverance; that they might obtain a better resurrection: And others had trial of cruel mockings and scourgings, yea, moreover of bonds and imprisonment: They were stoned, they were sawn asunder, were tempted, were slain with the sword: they wandered about in sheepskins and goatskins; being destitute, afflicted, tormented; (Of whom the world was not worthy:) they wandered in deserts, and in mountains, and in dens and caves of the earth. **And these all, having obtained a good report through faith, received not the promise.***
>
> HEBREWS 11:35-39

You will always find someone who will tell you, '*See there, some did not receive the promise so we are not all meant to receive promises and do exploits.*' Some people's ignorance is staggering! The promise that they did not receive was the coming of Christ in their day enabling the indwelling of the Spirit, which would make them partakers of the divine nature. They had all the types and shadows but never saw the fulfillment of His coming as the Redeeming Messiah. The author of Hebrews informed us that none of the Old Testament patriarchs received the promise, *'These all died in faith, not having received the promises, but having seen them afar off, and were persuaded of them, and embraced them, and confessed that they were strangers and pilgrims on the earth'* (Hebrews 11:13). They saw and embraced the coming of the redeeming Messiah by faith but never saw that promise in the flesh. And when they faced the decision to either reject God or accept death, they chose to accept death as a mark of their faith.

This in itself was a great exploit because they defied the tyrants of the day and the devil, with the view of receiving a better resurrection. The *better resurrection* is also applicable to us. Even though we are saved and indwelt by the Holy Spirit, for the moment we still do not have the culmination of our redemption, which is the glorified body. One of these days through the Blessed Hope when our Lord Jesus returns, something amazing will happen:

Behold, I shew you a mystery; We shall not all sleep, but we shall all be changed, In a moment, in the twinkling of an eye, at the last trump: for the trumpet shall sound, and the dead shall be raised incorruptible, and we shall be changed. For this corruptible must put on incorruption, and this mortal must put on immortality. So when this corruptible shall have put on incorruption, and this mortal shall have put on immortality, then shall be brought to pass the saying that is written, Death is swallowed up in victory. O death, where is thy sting? O grave, where is thy victory?

1 CORINTHIANS 15:51-55

We also await a better resurrection in that our bodies will be changed in a flash and we will possess a glorified body never to age, never to say, 'I used to be able to do that but I can't anymore'. These days will be over! Glory to God.

Barney E Warren was right when he penned this song in 1897:

Hallelujah, what a thought!
Jesus full salvation brought,
Victory, victory
Let the pow'rs of sin assail,
Heaven's grace can never fail,
Victory, victory.
Victory, yes, victory.

Hallelujah! I am free,
Jesus gives me victory;
Glory, glory! hallelujah!
He is all in all to me.

The exploit here was the denial of the tyrants wishes and their resolute faith in God, fulfilling what Jesus said:

For what is a man profited, if he shall gain the whole world, and lose his own.

MATTHEW 16:26

It is not that they did not receive the promised land and great victories, because they sure did. These men and women deliberately refused the deliverance of and from wicked tyrants in order to receive a better resurrection. They would not bow the knee to mortal men and although they did not receive at that time the indwelling of the Spirit in their spirit through the coming Messiah, God indwelt their conscience. They would rather deny the world, the flesh and the devil rather than denying God. That is an exploit!

CHAPTER 8
THE CONTRAST BETWEEN BELIEVING IN GOD AND BELIEVING GOD

THE reason so many believers are struggling to do exploits in the land is because of a lack of understanding of faith. This is why, as a believer once you are born again, the most important thing you need to know is how to live and operate by faith. Believing in God, in Christ or in Jesus does not necessarily mean living by faith. The world uses the term *'people of faith'* for people who believe in God. That refers to people of any religion who purportedly profess to believe in the existence of a supreme being. This includes all the major religions of the world and all the different groups that exist within Christianity such as the Methodist, Presbyterian, Lutheran, Baptist and Pentecostal, to name but a few. You know good and well that many who profess to believe in God and are supposedly people of faith are not living by faith. You will find first class doubters among these groups. In fact most of them do not even believe that miracles and healings can happen today. You don't have to go outside the church to find world class doubters, they are right there in church. Some of these world class doubters are even saved people in Pentecostal and Spirit filled churches. They are born again with their names written in the Lamb's book of life, on their way to heaven, but their days upon earth are marred with defeat and despair. Living a life of victory and doing exploits is not automatic simply because you are born-again or believe in God. Being born-again means that you are in Christ, which prepares you for heaven. But many who are in Christ are not in His Word or in faith. Jesus said:

If ye abide in me and my words abide in you...

JOHN 15:7

Everyone who is born-again is abiding in Christ but not everyone who is abiding in Christ has His words abiding in them. The master key to faith and dominion is to have His words resident in you. This is a deliberate act on your part. Now you can understand the saying, 'A person of faith does not necessarily mean he or she is living by faith.' It means he believes in God but does not necessarily believe God.

Everyone who is born-again is abiding in Christ
but not everyone who is abiding in Christ
has His words abiding in them

> What's the difference?

Some people do not think there is a difference, but there is and it is huge! To clarify this striking contrast we will look at Abraham, Luke and Paul. The New Testament emphatically brings this point across:

For what saith the scripture? Abraham believed God, and it was counted unto him for righteousness.

ROMANS 4:3

Even as Abraham believed God, and it was accounted to him for righteousness.

GALATIANS 3:6

And the scripture was fulfilled which saith, Abraham believed God, and it was imputed unto him for righteousness: and he was called the Friend of God.

JAMES 2:23

Three times we are deliberately being told that Abraham believed God which became a credit into his account as righteousness, labeling him as the friend of God. To be known as the friend of God, you have to believe God. There are many who believe *in* God but are not the friend *of* God. Here is the difference:

❖ Believing in God means I believe in the existence of God.

❖ Believing God means I go beyond believing in His existence and believe His Word to be the first and final authority in my life by acting on it.

The contrast is subtle but huge. To mark your thinking I will call it level 1 and level 2:

❖ Level 1 – Believing in God means I believe God exists.

❖ Level 2 – Believing God means I believe what He has said: His promises to be true and act I like it is so.

All born-again believers are in Level 1 but not all born-again believers are in Level 2. We should all be in Level 2 but many are just in Level 1. Let's look at some contrasting differences to locate where you are.

Level 1	Level 2
Believes in the existence of God	Believes in the existence of God and that He is a rewarder of those who seek Him
Believes in God	Believes in God and believes God's Word
Believers and unbelievers	Believers
Believes the days of miracles are passed away	Believes miracles are for today
Doubt, fear and unbelief	Faith, praise and victory
Believes the world above God	Believes the Word above the world
Circumstances dictate hope	God's promise dictates hope
Easily moved by the world	Easily moved by the Word
Believes the world cannot lie	Believes the Word cannot lie
The many voices speak volumes	Only God's voice matters
Moved by what is seen	Moved by what is unseen
Acts upon what the world says	Acts upon what the Word says

Anytime you believe any part of God's Word, it is credited to your account. Abraham believed God in respect to righteousness and it was put into his account. When you believe any of His promises they are put into your account to draw from. Let's look at a clear example of two believers in the same boat (literally) but with different attitudes. It will amply illustrate the contrast between believing *in* God and believing God:

> *But not long after there arose against it a tempestuous wind, called Euroclydon. And when the ship was caught, and could not bear up into the wind, we let her drive. And running under a certain island which is called Clauda, we had much work to come by the boat: Which when they had taken up, they used helps, undergirding the ship; and, fearing lest they should fall into the quicksands, strake sail, and so were driven. And we being exceedingly tossed with a tempest, the next day they lightened the ship; And the third day we cast out with our own hands the tackling of the ship. And when neither sun nor stars in many days appeared, and no small tempest lay on us, all hope that we should be saved was then taken away. But after long abstinence Paul stood forth in the midst of them, and said, Sirs, ye should have hearkened unto me, and not have loosed from Crete, and to have gained this harm and loss. And now I exhort you to be of good cheer: for there shall be no loss of any man's life among you, but of the ship. For there stood by me this night the angel of God, whose I am, and whom I serve, Saying, Fear not, Paul; thou must be brought before Cæsar: and, lo, God hath given thee all them that sail with thee. Wherefore, sirs, be of good cheer: for I believe God, that it shall be even as it was told me.*
>
> ACTS 27:14-25

Dr Luke, who was a traveling companion of Paul on his missionary journey wrote his second treatise to Theophilus – known as the book of Acts. He had first-hand experience into the life and ministry of Paul. The event above is Luke giving a brutally honest narration of what transpired when both of them were caught in a storm. He did not try to present himself in a good light as most people would. They were in the same ship heading to Italy for Paul to stand before Caesar when a catastrophic storm hit them. Paul had already warned them not to set sail as he perceived in his spirit that trouble was ahead but those in charge would not listen to him. Paul's inward witness soon played out before them as they were caught in a relentless, ruthless storm. It was a bad storm of the worst hurricane proportion, such that they lost control of the ship and from there things went from bad to worse.

Look at the words of Dr Luke, '*And we being exceedingly tossed with a tempest, the next day they lightened the ship; And the third day we cast out with our own hands the tackling of the ship. **And when neither sun nor stars in many days appeared, and no small tempest lay on us, all hope that we should be saved was then taken away**'* (Acts 27:18-20). Luke, who was in the same boat experiencing the same storm as Paul, came to the conclusion because he did not see the sun, moon and stars for many days that all hope that they could escape was gone. In fact Luke said, '*all hope that we should be saved was taken away.*' You cannot get any stronger a statement of doom and despair than that. Luke was seeing the end, failure and death. In his mind, this is where life ends – death by storm at sea.

On the other hand, Paul was in a different frame of mind. Look at his words:

...And now I exhort you to be of good cheer: for there shall be no loss of any man's life among you, but of the ship. For there stood by me this night the angel of God, whose I am, and whom I serve, Saying, Fear not, Paul; thou must be brought before Cæsar: and, lo, God hath given thee all them that sail with thee. Wherefore, sirs, be of good cheer: for I believe God, that it shall be even as it was told me.

ACTS 27:22-25

Two believers can be in the same boat having the same experience but with a different outlook and a different outcome

Luke was seeing doom, despair and death because he saw no moon, stars or sun and Paul was seeing deliverance and victory because he saw the Bright Morning Star and the Sun of Righteousness.

Were they believers? Yes, they were both believers in the same boat but in a different frame of mind.

Did Luke believe in God? Absolutely! However in this particular situation he did not believe God. Paul, on the other hand not only believed in God but took it further and believed God. Look at the words of Paul, '*Wherefore, sirs, be of good cheer: **for I believe God**, that it shall be even as it was told me.*' He believed God because he heard and had a promise from God. He believed what God said to him. Both believed in God but only one believed God. That does not mean that Luke was less saved than Paul. Nothing of the sort, but Paul was better equipped to deal with this particular situation because he had heard from God. Once you hear from God and believe Him, then that which is impossible becomes possible.

Jesus said unto him, If thou canst believe, all things are possible to him that believeth.

MARK 9:23

So my point to you is simply to go beyond the norm of saying 'I believe in God'. Millions of people say that and in fact look at what James says:

Thou believest that there is one God; thou doest well: the devils also believe, and tremble.

JAMES 2:19

You do well to believe in one God but you will do greater when you believe what that one God says and respond with corresponding actions.

*But wilt thou know, O vain man, that **faith without works is dead**? Was not Abraham our father justified by works, when he had offered Isaac his son upon the altar? Seest thou how faith wrought with his works,*

*and by works was faith made perfect? And the scripture was fulfilled
which saith, Abraham believed God, and it was imputed unto him for
righteousness: and he was called the Friend of God.*

JAMES 2:20-23

Faith without works is dead simply means *faith without corresponding
actions is fruitless.* It means our movements and comportment should match
what we say we believe. The true mark that I believe in God is that I believe
what He said and act upon it. Jesus said it this way:

And why call ye me, Lord, Lord, and do not the things which I say?

LUKE 6:46

*When I truly believe God, I do what He says and when I do what He
says I experience supernatural exploits.*

CHAPTER 9
APOKARADOKIA – INTENSE AND EARNEST EXPECTATION FOR EXPLOITS

IF ever there was a man who epitomized imposing, aggressive faith for exploits it was Paul the apostle. This man went through hell and high water and still came out smelling like roses. He did so because he knew God and believed God. When you read the book of Philippians you will discover that the central theme is joy. The key words in this epistle are *joy* and *rejoice* and yet in the natural there was nothing for Paul to rejoice or be joyful over as he was imprisoned when he wrote the epistle:

> *But I would ye should understand, brethren, that the things which happened unto me have fallen out rather unto the furtherance of the gospel; So that my bonds in Christ are manifest in all the palace, and in all other places; And many of the brethren in the Lord, waxing confident by my bonds, are much more bold to speak the word without fear. Some indeed preach Christ even of envy and strife; and some also of good will: The one preach Christ of contention, not sincerely, supposing to add affliction to my bonds: But the other of love, knowing that I am set for the defence of the gospel. What then? notwithstanding, every way, whether in pretence, or in truth, Christ is preached; and I therein do rejoice, yea, and will rejoice.*

> **For I know that this shall turn to my salvation through your prayer, and the supply of the Spirit of Jesus Christ, According to my earnest expectation and my hope,** *that in nothing I shall be ashamed, but that with all boldness, as always, so now also Christ shall be magnified in my body, whether it be by life, or by death. For to me to live is Christ, and to die is gain. But if I live in the flesh, this is the fruit of my labour:*

yet what I shall choose I wot not. For I am in a strait betwixt two, having a desire to depart, and to be with Christ; which is far better: Nevertheless to abide in the flesh is more needful for you. And having this confidence, I know that I shall abide and continue with you all for your furtherance and joy of faith;

PHILIPPIANS 1:12-25

Paul said that we should understand that the things which happened to him – meaning the imprisonment and the false brethren preaching to get him into trouble – did not stop the Gospel but helped to further it. Now when the Roman authorities had him in lockdown and the false brethren preaching to add to his troubles, the furtherance of the gospel was not their anticipation. They did so to stop the progress and advancement of the Gospel. Only a man with a spirit of faith can speak like Paul did. When he was put in lockdown, they did not expect that he would be released. As far as they were concerned, let's throw away the keys and let him rot in jail. Paul had a different idea. No matter what the world pronounces upon your life you cannot let them have the last word over you. Victory belongs to the one who has the last word.

Paul said, *'For I know that this shall turn to my salvation through your prayer, and the supply of the Spirit of Jesus Christ, According to my earnest expectation and my hope, that in nothing I shall be ashamed...'* (Philippians 1:19-20). Notice the words 'turn to' not 'turn against'. So many times people expect things to turn against them but in spite of the dire situation Paul expected things to turn for the better for him. He expected the best in a grow-worse situation. Paul said he expects things to *turn to his salvation*. What does that mean? The word salvation here cannot mean being born-again as Paul was already born-again and preaching the Gospel, hence his imprisonment. The Greek word for salvation here is *soteria* denoting deliverance and preservation. It is also used in the New testament to express the idea of sudden snatch from danger and evil circumstances. This verse in Greek reads as, 'I have perceived that this shall eventuate to my deliverance and my sudden snatching away from this impending danger.' In other words, Paul was saying, 'I know they have me all locked up and in lockdown; I know they've thrown away the keys expecting me to rot here but at any moment God will suddenly snatch me out of this mess.'

Always expect the best in a grow-worse situation

'*For I know that this shall turn to my salvation through your prayer, and the supply of the Spirit of Jesus Christ, According to my earnest expectation...*' Three things vital to being snatched away are prayer, the supply of the Spirit and expectation. Prayer is the demand and the Holy Spirit provides the supply which is the law of demand and supply. There can be no supply if there is no demand. Many wonder why there is no supply of the Spirit in their lives and that is because there is no demand made in prayer. You see the prayer that God cannot answer is the prayer that you don't pray. James told us, '*...ye have not because ye ask not...*' (James 4:3). Jesus also echoed the same sentiment:

> *And whatsoever ye shall ask in my name, that will I do, that the Father may be glorified in the Son. If ye shall ask any thing in my name, I will do it.*
> JOHN 14:13-14

The word ask here is also translated as demand and command one's due. God himself said, '*Ask me of things to come concerning my sons, and concerning the work of my hands command ye me*' (Isaiah 45:11). When you talk about imposing yourself upon God, you cannot get a clearer verse than this. God Himself tells us He expects us to appoint, command and impose ourselves upon Him. Why could Paul make such demand in prayer? Because he had earnest expectation.

〉 The intensity of earnest expectation

It is our expectation that determines our acquisition. This is not a 'wishy-washy kinda maybe perhaps one day in the sweet by and by' deal. Far from it!

wThis is an ardent and intense desire that will not retract until it sees the manifestation. Solomon sums it well in his writing, '*For surely there is an end; and thine expectation shall not be cut off*' (Proverbs 23:18). The Greek word for *expectation* is *apokaradokia* in Philippians and we want to look at its meanings. It is only used twice in the New Testament which, when deciphered into its context, will help us tremendously. Apokaradokia is used in Philippians 1:20 and in his Roman's epistle:

> *For I reckon that the sufferings of this present time are not worthy to be compared with the glory which shall be revealed in us. For the earnest expectation of the creature waiteth for the manifestation of the sons of God.*
>
> ROMANS 8:18-19

In both instances used, *apokaradokia* referred to a specific deliverance coming from a specific place with assurance. In Romans, Paul was expressing the sure hope every believer has in the redemption and reclothing of a glorified body. Whether the world likes it or not this is going to happen. One of these coming days corruption will take on incorruption. A glorified body which can never get old and never decay awaits every born again believer. What plastic surgery cannot do, the redemption of our bodies will do.

It is our expectation that determines our acquisition

The Vines Expository Dictionary of New Testament Words sheds much light on this word:

Apokaradokia is:

Primarily 'a watching with outstretched head' (*apo* meaning *from*; *kara* meaning the *head*; and *dokeo* meaning *to look, to watch*), signifies 'strained expectancy, eager longing'. The stretching forth of the head indicating an 'expectation' of something from a certain place.

The prefix *apo* suggests '*abstraction and absorption*' (Lightfoot), i.e. abstraction from anything else that might engage the attention, and absorption in the object expected 'till the fulfillment is realized' (Alford).

We will decipher the Vine's meanings with other meanings as well. Kenneth Wuest explains *Apokaradokia* as 'undivided and intense expectancy.' This speaks of total focus on the object desired. No distraction permitted. In his writing, Kenneth Wuest describes Apokaradokia as '*a person with head erect and outstretched, **whose attention is turned away from all other objects and riveted upon just one**. The word is used in the Greek classics of the watchman who peered into the darkness, eagerly looking for the first gleam of the distant beacon which would announce the capture of Troy.*' It is that concentrated, intense hope which ignores other interests and strains forward as with outstretched head. You know that you have tapped into apokaradokia when your attention for many distractions has veered and your mind is riveted on one object only.

Apokaradokia was also used describing the blinders or blinkers that horses wear during horse racing. It is a pair of small leather screens attached to a horse's bridle to prevent it seeing sideways and behind and being distracted from keeping its eyes and focus on the winning post. If you want to provoke unlimited exploits you will need to put on your spiritual blinders and not allow yourself to be easily distracted by what the devil or people are saying and doing. Here are three things we will look at:

❖ Stretched out head.
❖ Abstraction and absorption.
❖ Blinders preventing distraction.

❭ Stretched out head

Paul was saying, 'I may be in prison and all I can see in the natural are the four walls that has me in lockdown. But I have my head stretched out watching in anticipation to God to suddenly snatch me away from this imprisonment.' Faith is not moved by what it sees in the natural but what it can see from the spiritual. Irrespective of what the natural is saying as fact you can change it by '*looking unto Jesus the author and the finisher of our faith*' (Hebrews 12:2). How do I look unto Jesus? By looking unto His Word. Is your head stretched out looking for your miracle to show up or are you expecting the worst? So many believers do not walk with a stretched out head, indicating expectation that will not be cut off. They walk around with a sulking face and sunken shoulders. They would rather have a pity party sending invitations to every devil to attend. You know for sure the spirit of depression will be there first with his brother the spirit of failure. Lest we forget the spirit of murmuring will also be there and the spirit of bitterness, beside other despicable characters. Snap out of it! Stop feeling sorry for yourself! Get your expectation on. Get yourself some *apokaradokia*!

〉 Abstraction and Absorption

In essence Paul was saying, 'I am abstracting myself from anything negative that will engage my mind towards failure and I am fully absorbing myself in the thing desired.' He learned to abstract from the naysayers, the doubters and the enforcers of evil. He then absorbed himself with the constant thought of victory, miracles and deliverance. To absorb means to immerse in and drink, to soak in and suck, or to dip in order to amass. Like you would dip a sponge in water to absorb its content, which in this case is water, if you dip the sponge in blue dye it will drink in the blue dye and when you take it out it will be heavy with the content absorbed. If you were to press it with your finger, whatever content was absorbed when immersed would ooze out. Paul had so immersed himself in the Word of God and his spirit and mind became heavy with expectation of deliverance. So when pressed, the only thing that could come out is what was inside of him. Paul abstracted himself from anything and anyone that would engage his mind towards failure and absorbed himself in the promise that God would deliver him. He did not see the four walls or the closed door. All he saw was an open door and himself outside. He did not expect death but expected life.

> Put your blinders on

Paul had his blinders on like a horse in a race and would not be distracted by what was going on at his side and behind him. He only had his eyes on the winning post, which was freedom from prison and staying alive to further the faith of the Philippians' saints. What was the end result?

For I am in a strait betwixt two, having a desire to depart, and to be with Christ; which is far better: Nevertheless to abide in the flesh is more needful for you. And having this confidence, I know that I shall abide and continue with you all for your furtherance and joy of faith; That your rejoicing may be more abundant in Jesus Christ for me by my coming to you again.

PHILIPPIANS 1:23-26

But to remain in my body is more needful and essential for your sake. Since I am convinced of this, I know that I shall remain and stay by you all, to promote your progress and joy in believing,

PHILIPPIANS 1:24, 25 AMPC

This is a man where a death sentence was hanging over his life yet he chose not to die at that time. He said for him to remain alive was more beneficial for the Philippians so he decided that they would see him alive again. That was not the plan of the enemy! His plan was to get rid of Paul but Paul decided to hang around a little longer. This is what *apokaradokia* does. It is intense expectation that defies the devil. Rather than being exploited *apokaradokia* brings you to a place of supernatural exploits:

❖ Apokaradokia triggers exploits.
❖ Apokaradokia will disappoint the devil.
❖ Apokaradokia will bring life in a death situation.

Endnote

Vines Expository Dictionary of New Testament Words

Kenneth Wuest – Philippians In the Greek New Testament

CHAPTER 10
SEVENFOLD REVELATIONS OF FAITH – PART 1

I want to impact you with seven revelations of faith to revolutionize your walk with God to trigger unlimited exploits in your life. Once you grasp these seven understandings of faith, you will be unshakable and immovable.

1 FAITH IS THE PRESCRIBED LIFESTYLE OF THE RIGHTEOUS

As a born-again believer you have been justified by the blood of Jesus. Prior to you being born-again you lived your life the way you wanted to without a second thought. The day that you surrendered your life to Jesus you became *the just* which simply means *the justified one (just as if I never sinned)* or the one who has been declared righteous. Now that you are the just or the one declared righteous by the blood of Christ, how then should you live? What does God say about it? The question I asked myself when I gave my life to Jesus was, 'How do I live for God?' I was told a bunch of things that did not amount to much.

There are many who grew up in church and still did not know how to live for God. They knew how to live according to the precepts of their denomination but living for God was unknown. For others they thought they were living for God when they were into *dos* and *don'ts*, only to end up more frustrated with life.

> How do I live for God ?

> *I am crucified with Christ: nevertheless I live; yet not I, but Christ liveth in me: and the life which I now live in the flesh I live by the faith of the Son of God, who loved me, and gave himself for me.*
> GALATIANS 2:20

Look at the explicit words of Paul, '*The life that I now live in the flesh is by the faith of the Son of God.*' This is talking about now! Where you are right now, standing or sitting and breathing. As long as you are alive and not six feet under then you are living in the flesh, meaning in your body. Nonetheless while you are in your body and you are born-again you are to live by faith. Therefore faith is not something to use in times of emergency only but you are making it your lifestyle. Just like in the natural you live by breathing, you do not just breathe when you have an emergency. In fact if you don't breathe you will have an emergency. If you don't breathe then you are inviting death and in like manner if you don't live by faith then you are inviting death and disease. Apart from the above Scripture verse, the Bible reiterates the fact that the believer must live by faith. It is not optional:

But that no man is justified by the law in the sight of God, it is evident: for, The just shall live by faith.

GALATIANS 3:11

For therein is the righteousness of God revealed from faith to faith: as it is written, The just shall live by faith.

ROMANS 1:17

Now the just shall live by faith: but if any man draw back, my soul shall have no pleasure in him

HEBREWS 10:38

Behold, his soul which is lifted up is not upright in him: but the just shall live by his faith.

HABAKKUK 2:4

For we live by faith, not by sight.

2 CORINTHIANS 5:7 NIV

...Nevertheless when the Son of man cometh, shall he find faith on the earth?

LUKE 18:8

But without faith it is impossible to please him: for he that cometh to God must believe that he is, and that he is a rewarder of them that diligently seek him.

HEBREWS 11:6

You, the believer are under a mandate to live by faith. If you want to live for God then you live by faith; if you want to please God then you live by faith; if you want to be a true child of Abraham then you live by faith; if you want God to reward you then you live by faith; if you want to experience life as God wants you to experience it then you have to live by his prescribed way – Faith. Jesus asked the question, *'Nevertheless when the Son of man cometh, shall he find faith on the earth?'*

Will Jesus find faith in you?

Living for God is not a bunch of dos and don'ts
but simply living by faith

> What is living by faith?

I distinctly remember a sermon series when I was growing up and going to church. The man was teaching us on the subject of 'Walking in the Spirit.' The first Sunday, he taught us on the *importance* of walking in the Spirit. The second Sunday he taught us on the *benefits* of walking in the Spirit. By now my young mind was hungry and could not wait for the following week when he would tell us *how* to walk in the Spirit, only to be shown the consequences of *not* walking in the Spirit. I thought to myself , 'OK, now I know the importance of walking in the Spirit, the benefits of walking in the Spirit and what will transpire if I don't walk in the Spirit. Now next week I will get the final piece of the puzzle to give me the whole picture.'

I could not wait for the following Sunday, only to my disappointment he went on to a different subject. Millions of believers live with that kind of frustration because they are told they are to do certain things or live a certain way without ever being taught how to do it or what it is. So what do we mean when we say, 'Live by faith or walk by faith'? I will give you four definitions.

☙ Living by faith is living by the precepts, perspective and principles of God 's Word for the entire spectrum of your life

Living by faith is not just a way to get things from God but taking His Word and making it your lifestyle. In its simplest definition, living by faith is having confidence in the integrity of God's Word to act upon it.

Jesus said it this way, *'man shall not live by bread alone, but by every word of God'* (Luke 4:4).

☙ Living by faith is making God's Word the first and final authority in your life

Many believers have not made that decision. Instead, they have made their personal experiences the final authority in their lives. Our personal experiences do not validate God's Word. His Word is truth whether our experiences matches or not. You see, the whole universe revolves around the integrity of one verse:

> *God is not a man, that he should lie; neither the son of man, that he should repent: hath he said, and shall he not do it? or hath he spoken, and shall he not make it good?*
>
> NUMBERS 23:19

If this verse was ever to fail that is the day that God ceases to be God. It is impossible for God to lie (Hebrews 6:18). Today, we live in societies where lies are normal: politicians and the news media lie all the time and get away with it. Bosses lie to workers and adults to young ones. We can go on and on but just because we live in societies accustomed to lies does not mean that God is the same. God and His Word are one. It is His Word that makes Him God. His Word is unbreakable and unchangeable. In fact the Psalmist says:

For ever, O Lord, thy word is settled in heaven.

PSALM 119:89

Therefore living by the Word is living by a settled factor.

Making the Word the first and final authority in my life means I understand and know that God cannot lie

---

ℰ **Living by faith is living connected to the supernatural. It hooks you up to the anointing and is the door that gives God an opening to move in your life supernaturally**

The supernatural becomes a reality by the imposing force of faith. When the supernatural manifests, it imposes itself upon the natural, making the natural bow to its atmosphere. Jesus operated by faith and He superimposed supernatural onto the natural. Jesus operated by faith and the anointing. The people that came with faith made a demand upon the anointing. When faith and anointing collide, the supernatural manifests. It cannot manifest without faith. This is why living by faith is imperative. It is your connection to the supernatural and the miraculous.

ℰ **Living by faith is choosing to see life through the lens of God's Word rather than looking through your natural eyes**

Paul clearly told us, '*We walk by faith and not by sight*' (2 Corinthians 5:7). He also told the Corinthians saints:

While we look not at the things which are seen, but at the things which are not seen: for the things which are seen are temporal; but the things which are not seen are eternal.

2 CORINTHIANS 4:18

This verse lets us know that there are visible things and there are invisible things. There are things that we see and there are things that we do not see, yet they are there. What is unseen for us is not necessarily unseen for others. Paul casually told us not to look at things which are visible but invisible things. The question should be, 'How do I do that, Paul?' I know how to look at things which are visible by using my eyes. I have been doing this all my life. But how do I look at things which are invisible?

We are surrounded by invisible things on a daily basis. I am not just talking about angels and demons. How about germs and bacteria? We can't see them but they are there. They are invisible, meaning we not able to perceive them by our natural eyes. Invisible does not mean non-existent but simply means it is beyond the range of our eyes' capacity. There are stars that we see and stars beyond our sight's range that still exist, even thought we cannot see them with the naked eye.

> *Living by faith is the confidence to think, speak and*
> *act upon what God has said in His Word*

> Microscope, Telescope and Wordscope

What does *naked eye* mean? Here is the dictionary's definition – *Naked eye, also called bare eye or unaided eye, is the practice of engaging in visual perception unaided by a magnifying or light-collecting optical device, such as a telescope or microscope.* Since we cannot see germs with our naked eye what is it that enables us to see them? In order for us to see the germs or bacteria we would need an instrument called a microscope which enables the unseen to become seen. A microscope is an optical instrument used for viewing very small objects, such as mineral samples or animal or plant cells, typically magnified several hundred times. Therefore the microscope becomes the apparatus that helps us to see what we would consider the unseen realm. In like manner our naked eye can see a lot of far away stars at night without any instrument but there are some stars and planets that we cannot see with the power of the naked eye. This is why we use an apparatus known as a telescope. The word telescope is a combination of two words *tele* meaning *at a distance* and *scopium* meaning *scan, range* and *see*. Therefore when you combine these two words it means to see that which is at a distance. A telescope helps making that which is invisible to the naked eye to become visible. It does not manufacture the things in the unseen: these things are there already, the telescope, as well as the microscope are the aiding mechanism for us to see the reality of unseen things.

> How does this apply to you?

Just as the microscope and the telescope are the apparatuses making the already existent unseen things become seen, we also need an apparatus to see the already existent unseen things. This is how we fulfill the words of Paul to the Corinthians:

*While we **look not at the things which are seen, but at the things which are not seen**: for the things which are seen are temporal; but the things which are not seen are eternal.*

2 CORINTHIANS 4:18

I know with my naked eye I don't have the range to see already existent unseen things in the natural. How much more in the spiritual? Everything that you need or will ever need already exists in the unseen realm. Your victory, healing, deliverance, prosperity, promotion, breakthrough, anything you need. If you are sick you are looking to be healed. Jesus already paid and made healing available. In fact divine life is available to you right now, just as the planet Mars is available. In Mars' case you need a telescope or a rocket to view it. In your case you need the apparatus of God's Word. A microscope enables you to scope that which is micro (small) and make it visible. A telescope enables you to scope that which is tele (far) and make it visible. A Wordscope enables you to scope that which is in the Word (Bible promises) and make them visible. A microscope and telescope give sight to the unseen realities. The Wordscope gives sight to the new creation realities.

As a microscope and telescope give sight to unseen realities,
the Wordscope gives sight to the new creation realities

Therefore stop looking at life through the lens of your natural eyes and use the contact lens of the Word. The Scriptures are your contact lenses to your victory and anything else that you need. It is your contact with your healing, miracle and breakthrough. This is why I say to you living by faith is living by the lens or sight of God's Word. It is imperative for you to know that God's Word has sight:

> *For **the word of God** is quick, and powerful, and sharper than any twoedged sword, piercing even to the dividing asunder of soul and spirit, and of the joints and marrow, and is a discerner of the thoughts and intents of the heart. **Neither is there any creature that is not manifest in his sight: but all things are naked and opened unto the eyes of him with whom we have to do.***
>
> HEBREWS 4:12-13

In this verse, the subject being discussed is the Word of God. It is not the name of Jesus nor is it the blood of Jesus, as important as they are. The subject is not even God but the Word of God. So if I was to ask you these questions:

What is quick and powerful?
The Word of God

What is sharper than any two edged sword?
The Word of God

What can pierce even to the dividing asunder of soul and spirit, and of the joints and marrow, and is a discerner of the thoughts and intents of the heart?
The Word of God

So far so good! Now let me ask another question:

Whose sight is it that, 'Neither any creature that is not manifest in his sight: but all things are naked and opened unto the eyes of him with whom we have to do'?

Most people answer, 'God'. That is not the right answer. Remember the subject here is the **Word of God**. So how do we jump from answering all the questions with the answer, 'The word of God', only for the last question to be simply, 'God'? No! All the answers should be, 'The Word of God' as this is the subject. Clearly God is endeavoring for us to understand that His Word has sight. There are things which are open and naked to the sight of God's Word which are not to our natural eyes. Therefore if we want to see these things we must take on the sight of God's Word. Paul tells us, '*And the scripture, foreseeing that God would justify the heathen through faith...*' (Galatians 3:7-8). Therefore when you look at life through the lens of God's Word you are operating in foresight and not hindsight. The majority of the world – even in the church – operate in hindsight. You will often hear, 'If only I knew then what I know now'. Well why didn't you know? You can know when you operate through the foresight of God's Word. Looking at life through the spectacles of the Word removes you from being victimized by the elements of this world. Living by faith therefore empowers you to live above the elements of this world.

In its simplest definition living by faith is having confidence in the integrity of God's Word to act upon it

---

2 Faith is the mystery of mastery for the believer

Holding the mystery of the faith in a pure conscience.

1 Timothy 3:9

Faith is God's plan of dominion over all the works of the enemy. Your faith is the most potent force in the universe. John said, *'this is the victory that overcometh the world, even our faith'* (1 John 5:4). Faith is the mystery that gives you mastery over demons, diseases, delays, destruction, devastation and defeats. This is how the early church operated. This is how Jesus operated in the earth. He did so by faith! We know that Jesus walked by faith because the Father boomed out from heaven, *'This is my beloved Son in whom I am well pleased'* (Matthew 3:17). The only way we can please God is by faith (Hebrews 11:6) He dominated demons, diseases and devastations by faith.

Faith is the mystery that gives you mastery over demons, diseases, delays, destruction, devastation and defeats

---

〉 The object of our faith

Now that we know faith is the key to mastery in life, where exactly should our faith be? Faith is not the psyching up of yourself to believe that something positive will happen to you if you just muster up some belief. No! Faith has a specific place. So where should our faith be? We can all say that our faith must be in God and rightly so but in going through the Scriptures, there are three specific places our faith must be *in.*

ꙮ Faith in the blood which in essence is faith in the sacrifice of the Cross

Being justified freely by his grace through the redemption that is in Christ Jesus: Whom God hath set forth to be a propitiation through faith in his blood, to declare his righteousness for the remission of sins that are past, through the forbearance of God;

Romans 3:24-25

◔ Faith in the Word

Faith cometh by hearing and hearing by the Word of God

ROMANS 10:17

◔ Faith in the name of Jesus

And his name through faith in his name hath made this man strong, whom ye see and know: yea, the faith which is by him hath given him this perfect soundness in the presence of you all.

ACTS 3:16

This trinity of faith in the blood, the Word and the name of Jesus gives the believer a bloodline of authority, power and mastery over life.

3 FAITH IS AN ESTABLISHED LAW THAT WORKS FOR ANY BELIEVER IN ANY SITUATION

Where is boasting then? It is excluded. By what law? of works? Nay: but by the law of faith.

ROMANS 3:27

The law of faith is built on the premise of *believe and receive*. It is not the Old testament's futile ceremonial, moral, civil and Levitical laws to obtain righteousness. The reason they were futile is not because of the laws themselves but because no one could keep them due to the weakness of the flesh.

*What shall we say then? That the Gentiles, which followed not after righteousness, have attained to righteousness, even the righteousness which is of faith. **But Israel, which followed after the law of righteousness, hath not attained to the law of righteousness. Wherefore? Because they sought it not by faith, but as it were by the works of the law.** For they stumbled at that stumblingstone;*

ROMANS 9:30-32

Knowing that a man is not justified by the works of the law, but by the faith of Jesus Christ, even we have believed in Jesus Christ, that we might be justified by the faith of Christ, and not by the works of the law: for by the works of the law shall no flesh be justified.

GALATIANS 2:16

The law of faith is built on the premise of believe and receive

---

While the Levitical laws were built on the premise of *do and live* which came to *couldn't do and died*, the law of faith is simply, *believe you receive*.

Abraham believed God, and it was counted unto him for righteousness.

ROMANS 4:3

Abraham believed... And he received

ROMANS 4:3, 11

Jesus exposed and expressed the law of faith to the disciples showing it will work in any given situation – be it spiritual or physical:

For verily I say unto you, That whosoever shall say unto this mountain, Be thou removed, and be thou cast into the sea; and shall not doubt in his heart, but shall believe that those things which he saith shall come to pass; he shall have (receive) whatsoever he saith. Therefore I say unto you, What things soever ye desire, when ye pray, believe that ye receive them, and ye shall have them.

MARK 11:23-24

The law of faith is no respecter of persons. It does not look at color, race, age, nationality or sex. It is an established principle that is unchangeable, yet has the power to change your life.

Chapter 11
Sevenfold revelations of faith – Part 2

W<small>E</small> are looking into the sevenfold revelations of faith. When you grasp them they will bring you to a place of dominion. It is important for you to meditate upon these sevenfold definitions because if you get the basics right then the rest becomes easy. We have already looked at the previous three definitions, now let us look at the remaining four revelations.

4 Faith is a seed that can grow increasingly

For I say, through the grace given unto me, to every man that is among you, not to think of himself more highly than he ought to think; but to think soberly, according as God hath dealt to every man the measure of faith.

Romans 12:3

Every born-again believer has faith. According to the Apostle Paul we all have *the* measure of faith. That means the day that we were born-again we were given the same measure of faith as others who were born-again before us. Just like when you go to military basic training, everyone is given the same standard uniform and treatment, so it is when you enlist in the kingdom of God. Now, what you do with that measure once you have it determines how much it can grow:

If ye have faith as a grain of mustard seed, ye shall say unto this mountain, Remove hence to yonder place; and it shall remove; and nothing shall be impossible unto you.

Matthew 17:20

Every born again believer has the same standard measure of faith to begin – the seed measurement. What you do with it after that determines its potential to grow

---

The measure that we begin with is the seed standard. Peter said this in his epistle, *'Being born again, not of corruptible seed, but of incorruptible, by the word of God, which liveth and abideth for ever'* (1 Peter 1:23).

After that, just like a seed grows, your faith can grow. There are different stratums of faith in the Bible:

ὄ No faith

And that we may be delivered from unreasonable and wicked men: for all men have not faith.

2 Thessalonians 3:2

And he said unto them, Why are ye so fearful? how is it that ye have no faith?

Mark 4:40

ὄ Little faith

Wherefore, if God so clothe the grass of the field, which to day is, and to morrow is cast into the oven, shall he not much more clothe you, O ye of little faith?

Matthew 6:30

And immediately Jesus stretched forth his hand, and caught him, and said unto him, O thou of little faith, wherefore didst thou doubt?

Matthew 14:31

ὄ Great faith

Then Jesus answered and said unto her, O woman, great is thy faith: be it unto thee even as thou wilt. And her daughter was made whole from that very hour.

Matthew 15:28

When Jesus heard these things, he marvelled at him, and turned him about, and said unto the people that followed him, I say unto you, I have not found so great faith, no, not in Israel.

Luke 7:9

૯ Strong Faith

He staggered not at the promise of God through unbelief; but was strong in faith, giving glory to God;

ROMANS 4:20

૯ Weak Faith

And not being weak in faith, he did not consider his own body, already dead (since he was about a hundred years old), and the deadness of Sarah's womb,

ROMANS.4:19

Him that is weak in the faith receive ye, but not to doubtful disputations. For one believeth that he may eat all things: another, who is weak, eateth herbs.

ROMANS 14:1-2

૯ Unfeigned Faith

Now the end of the commandment is charity out of a pure heart, and of a good conscience, and of faith unfeigned:

1 TIMOTHY 1:5

When I call to remembrance the unfeigned faith that is in thee, which dwelt first in thy grandmother Lois, and thy mother Eunice; and I am persuaded that in thee also.

2 TIMOTHY 1:5

૯ Exceedingly Growing Faith

We are bound to thank God always for you, brethren, as it is meet, because that your faith groweth exceedingly, and the charity of every one of you all toward each other aboundeth;

2 THESSALONIANS 1:3

❭ Short Distance Faith

The more that you act upon God's Word, the more your faith will grow. The more your faith grows, the more experience you have. The more experience you have, the more hope for present and future situations you have and shame becomes a thing of the past. It is a domino effect. Now we know when we were born-again we all had the same measure of faith, so the more you hear the Word and act upon it the more your faith grows. When Jesus said to Peter (who was endeavoring to walk on the water to Him), '*O thou of little faith, wherefore didst thou doubt?*' (Matthew 14:31). The word *little* is better understood as *short distance*: Peter walked in short distance faith, whereas Jesus had long distance faith. Peter walked from the boat to Jesus and stumbled as he saw the boisterous wind. Jesus felt the same wind and yet walked from the shore all the way to the middle of the sea.

❭ Faith grows exceedingly

We all would love to go from *the* measure of faith to the long distance marathon faith, forgetting weak faith and going to strong faith, and best of all we all want exceedingly growing faith:

> *We are bound to thank God always for you, brethren, as it is meet, because that your **faith groweth exceedingly**, and the charity of every one of you all toward each other aboundeth; So that we ourselves glory in you in the churches of God for your patience and faith **in all your persecutions and tribulations that ye endure**:*
>
> 2 THESSALONIANS 1:3-4

Here's where the rubber meets the road! While we can be strong in faith by not staggering at the Word of God and be in long distance faith by keeping our eyes on Jesus, exceedingly growing faith is triggered in the patience of overcoming persecutions and tribulations. Now that doesn't mean that God is the one sending the tribulations, but in the world in which we live there are God haters and Paul describes them well in his epistle:

This know also, that in the last days perilous times shall come. For men shall be lovers of their own selves, covetous, boasters, proud, blasphemers, disobedient to parents, unthankful, unholy, Without natural affection, trucebreakers, false accusers, incontinent, fierce, despisers of those that are good, Traitors, heady, highminded, lovers of pleasures more than lovers of God;

2 TIMOTHY 3:1-4

We are living in days where the Gospel is mocked and the liberal media with liberal forces are endeavoring to remove God from society. While they mock and persecute, the church will stand and grow in faith exceedingly. You saw what happened in the early church in the book of Acts: the more they persecuted the church, the more of God's raw power manifested. Herod tried to kill Peter but the church prayed in faith and Herod was executed by the angel of the Lord with the following testimony:

But the word of God grew and multiplied.

ACTS 12:24

Whenever there was persecution, the church rose in faith and power and the Word of God prevailed. For exceeding problems, you need exceedingly growing faith to shut the mouth of the devil and his naysayers.

And many that believed came, and confessed, and shewed their deeds. Many of them also which used curious arts brought their books together, and burned them before all men: and they counted the price of them, and found it fifty thousand pieces of silver. So mightily grew the word of God and prevailed.

ACTS 19:18-20

While God doesn't send the persecutions, exceedingly growing faith is triggered in your patience of overcoming persecutions and tribulations of a wicked world at the behest of their wicked master, Satan

5 FAITH IS BEHIND THE VOICE OF THE SCRIPTURE

Behind every Scripture is the breath and the voice of God. Paul said, *'Every Scripture is God-breathed (given by His inspiration) and profitable for instruction, for reproof and conviction of sin, for correction of error and discipline in obedience, [and] for training in righteousness (in holy living, in conformity to God's will in thought, purpose, and action)'* (2 Timothy 3:16 Amplified Classic). Then he tells the Romans that faith comes by hearing and hearing the word of God, which in Greek is *rhema* meaning a spoken or quickened word. It didn't say faith comes by reading but by hearing. Reading sets you up to hear the voice of God in His Word. Solomon said, *'My son, attend to my words (meditating, reading and listening); incline thine ear unto my sayings(the Word becomes sayings and talks back to you or is quickened in you – breath and rhema)'* (Proverbs 4:20). I am sure this has happened to you. You were driving your car, minding your own business when all of a sudden a Scripture verse is quickened to your mind as you pondered over a situation. That quickened Word is his voice of inspiration to deliver you.

---

*Faith enables you to obtain a good report
in the sight of God*

---

6 FAITH IS A SPIRITUAL WEAPON

Faith is a spiritual weapon of mass destruction. It is both an offensive – as well as a defensive – weapon. In other words it is a weapon that protects you and a weapon that punishes the devil. Paul told the Ephesians saints:

Wherefore take unto you the whole armour of God, that ye may be able to withstand in the evil day...

EPHESIANS 6:13

The Lord has opened his armory and brought out weapons to explode his wrath upon his enemies...

JEREMIAH 50:25 (LIVING BIBLE)

God gave you His armor and in His armory is the weapon of faith with which you can do exploits in the camp of the enemy. As a believer you must understand the shielding aspect and the fighting aspect of faith:

Above all, taking the shield of faith, wherewith ye shall be able to quench all the fiery darts of the wicked

Ephesians 6:16

Fight the good fight of faith, lay hold on eternal life, whereunto thou art also called, and hast professed a good profession before many witnesses.

1 Timothy 6:12

The Greek word for shield is *thureos* which comes from *thura* meaning a door. Therefore the shield of faith is not the little round decorative shield called *apsis,* which is used in a victory procession, but *thureos* meaning that our shield of faith is as big as door to cover you from the top of your head to the tip of your toes. The Roman shield was drenched in water in order to quench all the fiery darts of the opposition. In like manner ours is drenched in the water of the Word to quench all the fiery darts of the wicked.

'*Fight the good fight of faith, lay hold on eternal life...*' (I Timothy 6:12). Faith fights to seize and lay hold of the superabundant life for you. We know grace has made all things available but it takes faith to access the grace of God. This is why Paul said, '*Therefore it is of faith, that it might be by grace; to the end the promise might be sure to all the seed*' (Romans 4:16). Without faith you frustrate the grace of God:

I do not frustrate the grace of God: for if righteousness come by the law, then Christ is dead in vain.

Galatians 2:21

Frustrate is *atheteō* meaning to thwart the efficacy of, nullify, and make void. Without faith we make void the grace of God thwarting its efficacy in our lives. It is as if He never shed the grace. Not that grace hasn't already been shed for everyone and for everything that pertains to life and godliness but it is as if it never was because we are not taking hold of it by faith. See what Paul wrote to Titus:

For the grace of God that bringeth salvation hath appeared to all men,
TITUS 2:11

The saving grace of God is available to all men but are all men saved? No! Now all men *can* be saved if they access the saving grace of God through faith, '*For by grace are you saved through faith.*' (Ephesians 2:5). Just the same, the healing grace, the prosperity grace and whatever grace you need are already at your disposal but you need to tap into the imposing faith that takes, in order for them to become a reality.

Without faith you frustrate the grace of God

---

7 FAITH HAS TO BE IN TWO LOCATIONS TO BE EFFECTIVE

*But the righteousness which is of **faith speaketh** on this wise, Say not in thine heart, Who shall ascend into heaven? (that is, to bring Christ down from above:) Or, Who shall descend into the deep? (that is, to bring up Christ again from the dead.) But what saith it? **The word is nigh thee, even in thy mouth, and in thy heart: that is, the word of faith, which we preach;** That if thou shalt confess with thy mouth the Lord Jesus, and shalt believe in thine heart that God hath raised him from the dead, thou shalt be saved. **For with the heart man believeth unto righteousness; and with the mouth confession is made unto salvation.***
ROMANS 10:6-10

We will look at this reality in more depth in the next chapter. This is a simple, powerful revelation that most of the church is oblivious to. For faith to be effective it must be in your heart and in your mouth. Whatever is in your heart in abundance will come out of your mouth. It is not enough for you to have the Word in your heart only, it must come out of your mouth. Remember the law of faith is 'believe and receive'. Well I believe with my heart and I receive the manifestation through my mouth's confession. Paul is very clear about it, 'Confession is made unto salvation.' The confession of your mouth is an expression of the belief of your heart which then becomes the constitution and possession of your life. With your ears you hear the Word, which becomes the word of faith which, when spoken becomes the established voice of victory over the world, the flesh and the devil. You will grasp a deeper understanding of the voice of faith in the next chapter.

The confession of your mouth is an expression
of the belief of your heart which then becomes
the constitution and possession of your life

CHAPTER 12
THE VOICE OF FAITH

GOD gave you a voice to overrule the verdict of the world and Satan. God gave you a voice to silence and overrule the bombardment of your mind. God gave you a voice to release victory in life. Satan is afraid of your voice and, more specifically the words that come out of your mouth through your voice. The way of exploits is through the voice of faith. When it comes to the voice of faith, two things are crucially important: God's Word and your words. There has to be synchronicity between your words and His Word. You must voice what He has already voiced.

❧ What do we mean when we say the voice of faith?

The voice of faith is simply you voicing the Word of God in the earth. It is the voicing of the promises of God over your problems. It is speaking the Promised Word to your mountains. The voice of faith is the voice of victory and dominion. You see, God's plan of dominion in the earth is through the voice of faith which is '*calling those things which be not as though they were*' (Romans 4:17). It comes from the spirit of faith which always receives and takes dominion in the name of Jesus. Your voice is the bridge between the natural and the supernatural.

We having the same spirit of faith, according as it is written, I believed, and therefore have I spoken; we also believe, and therefore speak;
2 CORINTHIANS 4:13

But what saith it? The word is nigh thee, even in thy mouth, and in thy heart: that is, the word of faith, which we preach; That if thou shalt confess with thy mouth the Lord Jesus, and shalt believe in thine heart that God hath raised him from the dead, thou shalt be saved.

For with the heart man believeth unto righteousness; and with the mouth confession is made unto salvation.

ROMANS 4:8-10

ঔ Faith must always be in two locations

One of the fundamental understandings you must possess in order to be effective in faith is to realize that faith must be in two places: in your heart and in your mouth. It's not enough to be just in your heart, it has also got to be in your mouth. With your heart you believe and with your mouth you voice or confess the promises of God. Paul declared that the spirit of faith believes and has a voice. Paul said, *'according as it is written, I believed, and therefore have I spoken; we also believe, and therefore speak;'* (2 Corinthians 4:13). Anything that speaks has a voice! Faith is not complete if you only believe: you must add your voice to your belief. To do anything, faith needs a voice. In the beginning, this world was created by the voice of faith:.

In the beginning God created the heaven and the earth. And the earth was without form, and void; and darkness was upon the face of the deep. And the Spirit of God moved upon the face of the waters. And God said, Let there be light: and there was light.

GENESIS 1:1-3

Through faith we understand that the worlds were framed by the word of God, so that things which are seen were not made of things which do appear.

HEBREWS 11:3

It is by faith that we understand that the universe was constructed by the Word of God, for the seen had to take its origin from the unseen.

BARCLAY'S NEW TESTAMENT

Faith is not complete if you only believe,
you must add your voice to your belief

God's voice of faith was the constructor of the universe. His voice of faith gave origins to all that became seen. I want you to understand the origins to all that became seen came through the mouth of God. The Spirit of God was hovering over the earth but nothing happened until God spoke.

If God did not speak, the Spirit would still be hovering today. God Himself operates through the voice of faith and when Jesus was on the earth He operated likewise. He voiced his faith to storms, the sea, the fig tree, sicknesses, death and deformities. Have you noticed when God spoke in Genesis, the Spirit moved and when Jesus voiced his faith, heaven backed him up?

For verily I say unto you, That whosoever shall say unto this mountain, Be thou removed, and be thou cast into the sea; and shall not doubt in his heart, but shall believe that those things which he saith shall come to pass; he shall have whatsoever he saith.

MARK 11:23

Satan is afraid of your voice and more specifically the words that come out of your mouth through your voice

The moment you begin to voice your faith, heaven will move on your behalf. Never hesitate to voice your faith in the midst of adverse circumstances. The devil would love for you to keep quiet because he knows that if you voice what God has already spoken about your situation it will drive him out:

* Sickness will be cast out.
* Depression will leave.
* Failure will be a thing of the past.
* Dominion and power will be a lifestyle.

It is through the voice of faith that God Himself did great exploits in the book of Genesis. If you want a new genesis in your life, your exploits will be through the voice of faith. This is a voice-activated system because God created it so. If you don't have the voice of faith then you will have the voice of circumstances and unbelief. Your voice is either your faith or fear speaking. Many have the voice of fear. Allow me to give you an acronym for fear:

Failure

Expected

And

Received

The voice of faith is simply you voicing the Word of God in the earth. It is the voicing of the promises of God over your problems. It is speaking the Promised Word to your mountains

---

ஃ The voice of faith

If you have the voice of fear, you will receive the failure anticipated. Now let's look closely at how the voice of faith works by looking at how God made it work:

For as the rain cometh down, and the snow from heaven, and returneth not thither, but watereth the earth, and maketh it bring forth and bud, that it may give seed to the sower, and bread to the eater: So shall my word be that goeth forth out of my mouth: it shall not return unto me void, but it shall accomplish that which I please, and it shall prosper in the thing whereto I sent it.

ISAIAH 55:10-11

God does not waste words but every time that He speaks, He expects His Word to be fully executed. From the book of Isaiah we are taught how God views the words of His mouth. '*So shall my word be that **goeth forth** out of my mouth: **it shall not return unto me void**... and prosper in the thing whereto I sent it*' Anytime that a word leaves or goes out of the mouth of God, He is sending His word and fully expects it to return. He does not expect that word to return to Him void but He expects it to return. Every Word of God has a **Return To Sender factor** to it. Every time God speaks He is sending His Word out, to come back to Him. Therefore God sees His word as a boomerang which goes and will return. Every word that God speaks has direction, destination and a mission to report back to Him. This is why God does not waste time with empty words. His words are purposeful and always on a mission. God sees His word as an apostle because he calls it the sent word. An apostle is a sent one, a commissioned one and one who executes a plan. As the centurion said to Jesus:

> *The centurion answered and said, Lord, I am not worthy that thou shouldest come under my roof:* **but speak the word only,** *and my servant shall be healed.* **For I am a man under authority, having soldiers under me: and I say to this man, Go, and he goeth; and to another, Come, and he cometh;** *and to my servant, Do this, and he doeth it. When Jesus heard it, he marvelled, and said to them that followed, Verily I say unto you, I have not found so great faith, no, not in Israel.*
>
> MATTHEW 8:8-10

That centurion had a revelation of the voice of faith. As a military man in command of one hundred soldiers, he understood the concept of sending soldiers on a mission to go and come back reporting after full execution. He understood that once his word is decreed, his soldiers obediently go as sent, commissioned ones to the battlefield and will return once the enemy has been defeated and the victory has been secured. In like manner he saw Jesus as the General that can send His word as a soldier to fully execute the healing of his afflicted servant. Jesus testified that this man had great and mega faith. Why? Because the centurion understood the apostleship of the Word of Jesus.

Every Word of God has a 'Return To Sender' factor to it

From today, see the Words of God as soldiers and commandos that go on a mission. His voice sent from heaven is a weapon of mass destruction into the camp of the enemy:

> *The Lord also **thundered in the heavens, and the Highest gave his voice;*** *hail stones and coals of fire. **Yea, he sent out his arrows, and scattered*** *them; and he shot out lightnings, and discomfited them.** Then the channels of waters were seen, and the foundations of the world were discovered at thy rebuke, O Lord, at the blast of the breath of thy nostrils. He sent from above, he took me, he drew me out of many waters. He delivered me from my strong enemy, and from them which hated me: for they were too strong for me. They prevented me in the day of my calamity: but the Lord was my stay. He brought me forth also into a large place; he delivered me, because he delighted in me.*
>
> PSALM 18:13-19

❯ Important point

Now it may look like the Word is being sent into a *Mission Impossible* scenario but when it gets back to God the report will be *Mission Accomplished*. Here is a very important point: God spoke His Word that it might be written and it was written so that it might be spoken. As long as the Word remains in the pages of the book, it will not do you any good. The moment you start declaring what you have read in the book, it will start working for you just as if God Himself was decreeing it. The Bible is called the Word of God, the Holy Scriptures, the Holy Writ and many other wonderful titles, but the moment you speak the Word of God it becomes the Word of faith:

> *But what saith it? The word is nigh thee, even in thy mouth, and in thy heart: that is, the word of faith, which we preach*
>
> ROMANS 10:8

> *So then faith cometh by hearing, and hearing by the word of God*
>
> ROMANS 10:17

The moment you hear the Word of God preached or taught it becomes the Word of faith, meaning you now have the potential to believe and act upon it. Do you remember what the author of Hebrews wrote?

For unto us was the gospel preached, as well as unto them: but the word preached did not profit them, not being mixed with faith in them that heard it.

HEBREWS 4:2

When you hear it preached or taught it becomes the Word of faith. You can latch your faith to the word that you have heard. When you believe it and speak it, you are mixing it with faith. When you then speak the Word that you have heard – mixing with your decision to believe and act upon it – it becomes the voice of faith. The moment the Word of faith becomes the voice of faith you then activate the 'Return To Sender' factor of Isaiah 54, only this time it is you who has sent the Word on a *Mission Impossible* and it will report back to you *Mission Accomplished*.

The moment the Word of faith becomes the voice of faith you then activate the 'Return To Sender' factor of Isaiah 54

The above paragraph is so important that I will re-insert it for you to grasp what was written. You need to get this understanding in your mind and spirit. As long as you don't hear it preached or taught, the Bible remains the *Word of God* or the *Holy Scriptures*. When you hear it preached or taught it becomes the **Word of faith**. When you then speak the Word that you have heard – mixing with your decision to believe and act upon it – it becomes the voice of faith. The moment the Word of faith becomes the voice of faith you then activate the 'Return To Sender' factor of Isaiah 54, only this time it is you who has sent the Word on a *Mission Impossible* and it will report back to you *Mission Accomplished*.

The voice of faith means your voice has become the voice of God. In God's case He literally voiced and sent His Word from heaven to earth. In your case, although you are presently on the earth, you also sent the Word from heaven because right now you are seated together in heavenly places in Christ Jesus. The Word of God is no respecter of persons: it will execute for you as it would execute for God. The day you realize that when you voice His Word, it is as if God Himself was speaking, your days of being hindered, obstructed and defeated will be over. God expects you to speak His Word to Him:

*Sing unto the Lord with the harp; with the harp, and the **voice of a psalm**.*
PSALM 98:5

The voice of the Psalm is the voicing of His Word back to Him. Have you ever heard someone say this about a person: 'He loves the sound of his own voice' meaning the person likes to talk and talk? In reality, God loves the sound of *your* voice, especially when you voice *His* Word and promises. On the other hand, Satan hates your voice, especially when you voice the Word of God; then, he can no longer exploit you but you can exploit him. Let us briefly look at the effects of the voice of God from the Psalmist and Isaiah:

The voice of the Lord is upon the waters: the God of glory thundereth: the Lord is upon many waters. The voice of the Lord is powerful; the voice of the Lord is full of majesty. The voice of the Lord breaketh the cedars; yea, the Lord breaketh the cedars of Lebanon. He maketh them also to skip like a calf; Lebanon and Sirion like a young unicorn. The voice of the Lord divideth the flames of fire. The voice of the Lord shaketh the wilderness; the Lord shaketh the wilderness of Kadesh. The voice of the

Lord maketh the hinds to calve, and discovereth the forests: and in his
temple doth every one speak of his glory.

PSALM 29:3-9

For through the voice of the Lord shall the Assyrian be beaten down,
which smote with a rod.

ISAIAH 30:31

The voice of him that crieth in the wilderness, Prepare ye the way of the
Lord, make straight in the desert a highway for our God. Every valley
shall be exalted, and every mountain and hill shall be made low: and
the crooked shall be made straight, and the rough places plain: And the
glory of the Lord shall be revealed, and all flesh shall see it together: for
the mouth of the Lord hath spoken it.

ISAIAH 40:3-5

The voice of the Lord thunders and removes powerful opposition; it prepares the way, making a highway in the desert, leveling the battlefield and reveals the glory of God. As you release the voice of faith you prepare for God to move in your life and you will see the glory of God.

With your ears you hear the Word which becomes the word
of faith which when spoken becomes the voice of faith which
becomes the established voice of victory over the world,
the flesh and the devil

The voice of faith is God's plan of dominion for you to eradicate defeat, delays, despair, destruction and devastation. If you are serious about shedding the defeat cycle from your life to start living in the victory cycle, it is imperative that you to live by the voice of faith. The words we speak from our mouths are very important. A believer has no business saying whatever comes to his mind.

God's Holy Word has a lot to say about our words and how they affect us:

Thou art snared with the words of thy mouth, thou art taken with the words of thy mouth.

PROVERBS 6:2

You are taken as in a net by the words of your mouth, the sayings of your lips have overcome you.

BBE

A man's belly shall be satisfied with the fruit of his mouth; and with the increase of his lips shall he be filled. Death and life are in the power of the tongue: and they that love it shall eat the fruit thereof.

PROVERBS 18: 20-21

God spoke His Word that it might be written and it was written so that it might be spoken

---

> Take words

Never go to God with an empty mouth. Jesus is the high priest and executor of your words before the Father. An apostle was one sent on a mission to execute the decree:

Take with you words, and turn to the Lord: say unto him...

HOSEA 14:2

Wherefore, holy brethren, partakers of the heavenly calling, consider the Apostle and High Priest of our profession, Christ Jesus

HEBREWS 3:1

Thou shalt also decree a thing, and it shall be established unto thee: and the light shall shine upon thy ways.

JOB 22:28

When you go before God you have to take words. Hosea said '*take with you words...*' What kind of words? Faith-filled words to be exact. Go before God with the voice of faith. He responds to words – more specifically His Word. If a man ever goes to God with the Word of God in his mouth, it is as if Jesus Himself was standing before the Father. As the Father would respond to Jesus, He will respond to you. Don't take whining and doubts before Him – that will not activate him. Words of fear and doubt activate Satan and words of faith activate God; He is a faith activated God; He is a Word-Activated God (His Word in your mouth). I take the Word of Almighty God before my heavenly High Priest, Jesus. In the Old Testament, whether one person, a priest, a high priest or a number of people went before God, they did so with a sacrifice. No one could approach God without a sacrifice. Today the sacrifice that we bring is the fruit of our lips:

> *By him therefore let us offer the sacrifice of praise to God continually, that is, the fruit of our lips giving thanks to his name.*
>
> HEBREWS 13:15

> *I create the fruit of the lips...*
>
> ISAIAH 57:19

The sacrifices that we make today for our Heavenly High Priest to bring before God are the fruit of our lips. God then will create the fruit of your lips. This is why Solomon said, '*A man's belly shall be satisfied with the fruit of his mouth; and with the increase of his lips shall he be filled*' (Proverbs 18:20). The fruit that will taste good to your palette and life are the ones that God creates. The fruit that will taste bad to your palette are the words that empower Satan to move against us. You must be aware of the words of your mouth. You must understand that words are containers; they are filled with things or forces. Have you ever heard someone say, '*It was just empty words*'? There are no such things as empty words! Words are filled with joy and victory or they can be filled with all kinds of negativity. Whether we like it or not we are subject to words. The sooner we realize this, then the sooner we will carefully choose the words we speak about ourselves and situations of life. Many people look back over the years and ruminate over the things they have done or what they haven't done. I also believe that we should ponder upon what we have said and didn't say. You see, what you *did* came through what you *said* and uttered; your words were the connection between what you *believed* and *received*. It may seem unimportant to you but words are actually spiritual triggers that will produce great explosions in your life. For untold amounts of believers, Satan has tricked them into using that trigger power against themselves. King David compared words to arrows. In speaking about the wicked he said of them:

> *who sharpen their tongues like swords and aim their words like deadly arrows*
>
> PSALM 64:3 NIV

> *Who make their tongues sharp like a sword, and whose arrows are pointed, even bitter words*
>
> BBE

Think about the analogy of the sword and arrows compared to words, signifying they are lethal weapons. A sword or arrow will either work for or against you. An arrow or bullet will simply go where it is pointed. It will not change its direction once it is triggered or released but it will hit its designated target. That's exactly how words function, they go in the direction that you release them. Once you voice your thoughts they go toward a designated target and they never miss:

> *The heart of the righteous studieth to answer: but the mouth of the wicked poureth out evil things.*
>
> PROVERBS 15: 28

> *Heaviness in the heart of man maketh it stoop: but a good word maketh it glad.*
>
> PROVERBS 12:25

Notice the writer said, 'a good word' makes your heart strong and the righteous studies before he speaks. The apostle James instructed us in his epistle to be '*slow to speak*' (James 1:19). That's how you will avoid calamities and disasters from being the norm in your life. Some people need to learn the vocabulary of silence: if you are not saying anything negative you are not triggering anything bad to shoot yourself in the foot. We have to watch what we say. In fact the Word tells you what to say or speak:

If any man speak, let him speak as the oracles of God...

1 PETER 4:11

If anyone has anything to say, let it be as the words of God...   BBE

You can change the course of your life today with the voice of faith. As you learn the principles of the Word of God and voice your faith, you will blast through the mountains of failures and get to the victory side in this life and the life to come. Speak God's Word only! No matter what the devil or the circumstance say. You cannot be healed if you keep voicing sickness and death: God Himself cannot get you healed because He will not break the law of faith, as stated in the gospel of Mark by Jesus:

...he shall have whatsoever he saith

MARK 11:23

Your turning point in your life will begin when you have a turning point in your mouth and heart. The Apostle Paul declared, '*The word is nigh thee, even in thy mouth and in thy heart*' (Romans 10: 8). The Word that you have in your heart – that is voiced through your mouth – will dominate the world, the flesh and the devil. It will make you the governor of your life, according to the Apostle James:

Behold also the ships, which though they be so great, and are driven of fierce winds, yet are they turned about with a very small helm, whithersoever the governor listeth.

JAMES 3:4

The voice of faith makes you the governor over demons, principalities and powers; it is the voice that cannot and will not be denied. Sometimes it may look like it is being denied, but it is not. Don't be moved by what you see or feel, just keep speaking the Word and *voice your faith*. The Word of God – through your voice – will activate the supernatural, creating signs and wonders:

God thundereth marvellously with his voice; great things doeth he, which we cannot comprehend.

JOB 37:5

And it shall come to pass, if they will not believe thee, neither hearken to the voice of the first sign, that they will believe the voice of the latter sign.

EXODUS 4:8

Notice that God calls the voice signs. The voice of faith creates signs and wonders, does great things and reveals the Glory of God.

Because all those men which have seen my glory, and my miracles, which I did in Egypt and in the wilderness, and have tempted me now these ten times, and have not hearkened to my voice.

NUMBERS 14:22

And ye said, Behold, the LORD our God hath shewed us his glory and his greatness, and we have heard his voice out of the midst of the fire: we have seen this day that God doth talk with man, and he liveth.

DEUTERONOMY 5:24

The voice of faith is the voice of triumph; the voice of faith will make you see the glory of God. It will bring healing, deliverance, prosperity and protection over your life. Just as the Word of God will not go back void to God, the voice of faith will not come back void to you. Speak the Word! Jesus is the executor of your confession. He will execute your words of faith. What are you voicing for him to execute?

Wherefore, holy brethren, partakers of the heavenly calling, consider the Apostle and High Priest of our profession, Christ Jesus

HEBREWS 3:1

Many believers say, 'It doesn't seem that the Lord has done anything for me lately.' The problem is not with the Lord, it is your mouth: either you are keeping it shut or when you open it you blabber unbelief.

Open your mouth and voice God's Word. That is your ticket to great exploits and victory.

The voice of faith makes you the governor over demons, principalities and powers. It is the voice that cannot and will not be denied

---

CHAPTER 13
EXPLOITS THROUGH PERSISTENT AND IMPORTUNATE PRAYER

IT is important to know that great exploits come from the exploits of great prayers. Prayer and exploits go together just as faith and exploits do because they are synonymous: the exploits of faith are the exploits of prayer. Many have tried to separate prayer and faith but in reality, prayer is an expression of your faith and faith is released through prayer. They work hand in hand. Prayer is not more important than faith and faith is not more important than prayer. They are mutually important. Is the bullet more important than the gun or are they mutually important? They are mutually important as one is ineffective without the other. When both come together they create an explosion. There will be an explosion of exploits in your life when you pray. The people who have seen great exploits have been those who faithfully prayed, with persistent and importunate prayers. It takes the brand of imposing, aggressive faith to persist in prayer when all the demons of hell are opposing you.

One crucial thing to understand is that although there are many types of prayers in the Bible, all of them are expressions of the prayer of faith. I realize that we have used the term 'the prayer of faith' from the book of James and somehow solely connected the prayer of faith to Mark 11:23-24 but in reality all types of prayer – whether it is the prayer of agreement, the prayer of binding and loosing, intercession, supplication, confession, importunate prayer and petition – all operate on the premise of faith. All prayers are the prayer of faith otherwise they will not work. You cannot intercede without faith and you cannot do the prayer of agreement in unbelief. Each type of prayer is done through faith.

You and I, as a family members of the house of God, have a calling of prayer over our lives. The word *house* in Greek is *oikos* meaning *family*:

> *And he taught, saying unto them, Is it not written, My house shall be called of all nations the house of prayer? but ye have made it a den of thieves.*
>
> MARK 11:17

Although there are many types of prayers in the Bible,
all of them are expressions of the prayer of faith

As a member of the family, prayer is not optional but essential: it is our call. We must become proficient in prayer. As I just mentioned there are many types of prayers in the Bible – and volumes have been written about them. In our study, we will look at the efficacy of persistent and importunate prayer for exploits.

> *And he said unto them, Which of you shall have a friend, and shall go unto him at midnight, and say unto him, Friend, lend me three loaves; For a friend of mine in his journey is come to me, and I have nothing to set before him? And he from within shall answer and say, Trouble me not: the door is now shut, and my children are with me in bed; I cannot rise and give thee. I say unto you, Though he will not rise and give him, because he is his friend, **yet because of his importunity he will rise and give him as many as he needeth.** And I say unto you, Ask, and it shall be given you; seek, and ye shall find; knock, and it shall be opened unto you. For every one that asketh receiveth; and he that seeketh findeth; and to him that knocketh it shall be opened.*
>
> LUKE 11:5-10

Jesus was teaching the disciples, who asked Him to help him develop his prayer life. After going through what is known as the Lord's prayer, he narrated the above account to illustrate to us the power of importunate and persistence in prayer. We will couple this story with another story that Jesus narrated to fully grasp the prayer of importunity:

> *And he spake a parable unto them to this end, that men ought always to pray, and not to faint; Saying, There was in a city a judge, which feared not God, neither regarded man: And there was a widow in that city; and she came unto him, saying, Avenge me of mine adversary. And he would not for a while: but afterward he said within himself, Though I fear not God, nor regard man; Yet because this widow troubleth me, I will avenge her, lest by her continual coming she weary me. And the Lord said, Hear what the unjust judge saith. And shall not God avenge his own elect, which cry day and night unto him, though he bear long with them? I tell you that he will avenge them speedily. Nevertheless when the Son of man cometh, shall he find faith on the earth?*
>
> LUKE 18:1-8

Pay attention to these words, '*And he spake a parable unto them to this end, that men ought always to pray, and not to faint...*' The purpose of this parable was to illustrate that we must always be persistent and never give up in prayer. Persisting in prayer is not a lack of faith but a *whack* of faith against opposition, doubt and the devil. Both of these accounts show us the exploits of importunate prayer.

Prayer is not optional but essential: it is our call

♭ What is importunate prayer?

This is not commonly heard in the modern church. Importunate prayer is persistent prayer that will not give up until the answer manifests. Importunity is *shameless confidence,* in the midst of a shameful situation. 'Importunate – persistent – shameless confident' prayer is needed to defy the antagonism and hostile obstruction to your destiny.

⌘ The widow and the unjust judge

I first want to look at the case of the widow woman and the unjust judge, then we will look at the midnight friend. This woman was a widow, which indicates her husband had died. For her to go to a judge reveals a legal problem. Not every widow goes to a judge when their husband dies. This indicates that either her husband was murdered or after his death what was due to her was withheld. Any which way, she felt a sense of injustice against her. Her first words to the unjust judge were, 'Avenge me of mine adversary.' Newer renditions of this verse say, 'Give me justice against my adversary.' She felt a sense of injustice because her husband was taken away from her and her legal dues were being opposed and withheld.

---

*Importunity is shameless confidence
in the midst of a shameful situation*

It is interesting that she engaged the word adversary which, in Greek is *antidikos*, a combination of two words, *anti* and *dikos*. *Anti* simply means to deny, or against and *dikos* means right. So when you combine the two words they mean to deny your rights. Her adversary was denying her rights. Peter rips the cover in his epistle and lets us know who our adversary is, *'Be sober, be vigilant; because your adversary the devil, as a roaring lion, walketh about, seeking whom he may devour'* (1 Peter 5:8). The devil is your adversary and he will deny you your legal rights. Just because something belongs to you does not mean that he will not obstruct justice in your life. That woman kept going before the unjust judge and would not budge until her request was granted. Her shameless, continual going broke the unjust judge's iron will and made him compliant to her request in granting her justice. God is not the unjust judge but the righteous judge, as Abraham revealed to us:

Shall not the Judge of all the earth do right?

Genesis 18:25

God is a righteous judge, who wants to bring justice to you speedily. Listen to what Jesus said, '*And shall not God avenge his own elect, which cry day and night unto him, though he bear long with them? I tell you that he will avenge them speedily. Nevertheless when the Son of man cometh, shall he find faith on the earth?*' (Luke 18:7-8). I really like this rendition of these verses from another translation:

> *And the Lord said, "Listen to what the unrighteous judge says! Won't God give justice to his chosen ones, who cry out to him day and night? Will he delay long to help them? I tell you, he will give them justice speedily. Nevertheless, when the Son of Man comes, will he find faith on earth?"*
> LUKE 18:7-8 NEW ENGLISH TRANSLATION

God is the righteous judge, who wants
to bring justice to you speedily

God will not delay your justice but will grant it speedily as you call upon Him day and night in imposing, aggressive faith. You see, the reason why we tap into importunate prayer is not because God is holding out against us but because we have an enemy that endeavors to put stumbling blocks in our lives. Therefore we have to contend in battle – in prayer. See this example in the Old Testament that sheds light on our predicaments today:

> *Rise ye up, take your journey, and pass over the river Arnon: behold, I have given into thine hand Sihon the Amorite, king of Heshbon, and his land: begin to possess it, and contend with him in battle*
> DEUTERONOMY 2:24

God said to His people, '*I have given into your hand the land but you must contend in battle for it.*' Why do I have to contend for what God has already given me? Because there was an occupier of that land that needed to be dislodged. Right now you need to understand there is an occupant in your Promised Land that needs to be evacuated so you can move in. He will not leave easily. This is why we contend in faith and in prayer. Today we contend in battle by importunate prayer that will not surrender and quit until we see the manifestation of our Promised Land. That widow wearied the unjust judge who was holding out justice for her. You will hound the devil and his cohorts until they leave your property, and God the righteous Judge will back you swiftly. Your problem is not God: He is your answer; He is the one that will back you up when you are relentless. Always remember what James and Peter said to us:

Resist the devil, and he will flee from you.

JAMES 4:7

Be sober, be vigilant; because your adversary the devil, as a roaring lion, walketh about, seeking whom he may devour: Whom resist stedfast in the faith, knowing that the same afflictions are accomplished in your brethren that are in the world.

1 PETER 5:8-9

James said to resist the devil and Peter informed us that we do so by faith. Never forget that when you persist against the devil you break his resistance. When you persist in prayer and in faith you will break the resistors of your destiny. Many of today's believers give up too easily. They have no mettle in their prayer lives. They are soft, emotional, situation-driven believers that do not have a back-bone in the Word, prayer and faith. The devil loves soft ground that he can easily manipulate. He looks for those he *may* devour meaning there are those he *may not* devour. The ones he may not devour are those who will persist day and night in importunate prayer. For every prophecy you have ever received you have to contend for it in prayer. For every vision that God ever gave you, they will not be fulfilled automatically. You have to contend in importunate prayer. The old timers used to call it 'Praying through'.

We contend in battle by importunate prayer that will not surrender and quit until we see the manifestation of our Promised Land

---

I will never forget how I reacted when I was reading the book of Isaiah while I was on a trip to Accra, Ghana. What I read that day shook me up for the better – but it shook me up. I threw my Bible on the bed and said to God, 'Lord if what you are saying is true then you are in trouble with me.' I picked up my Bible again and read that verse and threw my Bible again on the Bed, 'Lord if this is true and I know it is then you are in trouble with me.' What did I read specifically?:

I post watchmen on your walls, O Jerusalem; they should keep praying all day and all night. You who pray to the Lord, don't be silent! Don't allow him to rest until he reestablishes Jerusalem, until he makes Jerusalem the pride of the earth.

ISAIAH 62:6-7

Watchmen are intercessors and prayer warriors. God said, 'You who call upon my name in prayer, keep not silent and don't give me any rest until I establish you and make you the praise and pride of the earth.' You have an open invitation from God to never relent in prayer but to persist in prayer until you are established and become a praise in the earth. This is why I said to God, 'You are in trouble with me, I will not be silent. I will be like Jacob that said, I will not let you leave until you bless me.' Do you have that kind of intensity in prayer? You need to come to the place where both God and the devil know where you stand. Both God and the devil must see that you are not a quitter. When God sees your tenacity, He enforces your justice and when Satan sees your tenacity, he lets go of your possession. Now let's go to Jesus' parable of the midnight friend:

And he said unto them, Which of you shall have a friend, and shall go unto him at midnight, and say unto him, Friend, lend me three loaves; For a friend of mine in his journey is come to me, and I have nothing to set before him? And he from within shall answer and say, Trouble me not: the door is now shut, and my children are with me in bed; I cannot rise and give thee. I say unto you, Though he will not rise and give him,

*because he is his friend, **yet because of his importunity he will rise and
give him as many as he needeth.** And I say unto you, Ask, and it shall
be given you; seek, and ye shall find; knock, and it shall be opened unto
you. For every one that asketh receiveth; and he that seeketh findeth;
and to him that knocketh it shall be opened.*

LUKE 11:5-10

This is a story to inform us to keep on and persist in prayer. Jesus set the
scene for us: a man (whom we will call Joe) had a friend (whom we will
name Phil) who came to visit him at midnight and Joe had nothing to give
to Phil. Although he had nothing, Joe had another friend (whom we will
name Brian) whose home he went to knock on the door of at midnight to
ask for bread. Brian was indeed the friend of Joe, but because of the lateness
of the hour, spoke from within his house and said, 'My wife is sleeping, my
kids are sleeping, as is my dog, so I cannot rise and give you bread.' That
did not deter Joe in the least bit: he did not care that it was midnight; he did
not care that he would inconvenience Brian – who was tucked up in bed,
sleeping soundly. Joe had shameless confidence and the audacity to impose
upon his friendship with Brian to get what he needed to be able to help Phil.

---

*When God sees your tenacity he enforces your justice and
when Satan sees your tenacity he lets go of your possession*

---

৫ Our dilemma

Many times we find ourselves in the same situation as Joe or the man in
the parable, when his friend comes to him at an inconvenient time with
a problem and we have nothing to give to him. We feel helpless because
someone has come with a need and we have nothing in our arsenal to help
them. However that's not the end of the matter. Just like Joe had another
friend, we also have another friend when we don't have anything to give
to someone in need: we go to our friend, Jesus. He is the friend that sticks
closer than a brother. Going back to our Joe, Phil and Brian scenario again,

we see an important lesson. Phil went to Joe and Joe went to Brian. So in all this Joe is the middle-man that takes from Brian to meet the need of Phil. This makes Joe (being in the middle) an intercessor. Many times we have nothing physically to give our friends and loved ones but we can be in the middle, with intercessory and relentless prayer. You can go to the Lord on behalf of a loved one or a friend. The greatest thing you can give to a loved one is your non-stop, relentless prayer that will break their problems and meet their needs.

⟩ Because of his importunity

We have already discovered that importunity means shameless confidence. Importunate prayer is prayer that will persist and break every antagonism of the enemy. I want to give you eight awesome secrets of importunate prayer:

❖ Importunate prayer is the art of dealing and appealing to the friendship of God on behalf of another friend. We see this in the parable: the man goes to his friend at midnight on behalf of his other friend.

❖ Importunate prayer is a shameless and inconvenient urgency that persists in request and petition until it is granted.

❖ Importunate prayer engages 'asking, seeking and knocking' until the answer manifests. Asking is *petitioning*, seeking is *supplicating* and knocking is *interceding*. It moves through these dimensions of prayer to obtain its objectives.

❖ Importunate prayer is prayer that grows in intensity, perseverance and tenacity.

❖ Importunate prayer is not bothered by the 'passed time' or 'too late' factor. The 'too late' factor is not even a factor; it just goes and gets the job done.

❖ Importunate prayer is prayer that is relentless until it receives.

❖ Importunate prayer is the effectual, fervent prayer of the righteous that makes tremendous power available, to ensure that justice is rendered.

❖ Importunate prayer is prayer that possesses the gates of your enemies, dethroning principalities.

The words importunate, importunity, opportune and opportunity have the same etymology: *Portus,* meaning harbor. Opportunity is from the Latin word *opportunus*, from *ob-* 'in the direction of' and *portus-* 'harbor' originally describing the wind driving toward the harbor, hence 'seasonable.' Importunity is from the Latin word importunus meaning 'inconvenient, unseasonable,' based on Portunus, the name of the god who protected harbors (from portus 'harbor').

OXFORD ENGLISH DICTIONARY.

So when we tap into the prayer of importunity we are removing the god of gates and harbors – that commands what comes in and goes out. Many times in our lives, things that should be coming in are not coming in and what should be leaving are not leaving. It can happen on a personal, familial and national level. So it looks like we are constantly out of season. Importunate prayer makes that which is out of season to be in season. Jericho was a prime example of a stronghold of no one coming in and going out. Look at the words of Moses:

> *And we took all his cities at that time, there was not a city which we took not from them, threescore cities, all the region of Argob, the kingdom of Og in Bashan. **All these cities were fenced with high walls, gates, and bars; beside unwalled towns a great many.** And we utterly destroyed them, as we did unto Sihon king of Heshbon, utterly destroying the men, women, and children, of every city. But all the cattle, and the spoil of the cities, we took for a prey to ourselves.*
>
> DEUTERONOMY 3:4-7

The walls, bars and gates were destroyed and they took the spoil of the cities. Through importunate prayer you will destroy the walls, bars and gates and take the spoil. God is no respecter of persons; He will back you up. Great exploits come from importunate prayer. It takes shameless, boldface faith to persist in prayer. Keep praying and you will defy the odds and win.

Importunate prayer is prayer that possesses the gates of your enemies, dethroning principalities

---

CHAPTER 14
EXPLOITS THROUGH THE LEADING OF THE SPIRIT

IT is vitally important – if we want to provoke unlimited exploits – that we know the leading of the Spirit. If a man is well acquainted with the Holy Spirit and knows how to receive direction from Him, exploits will be the order of the day. Being led by God is the privilege and the right of every believer, but too many are living below their privileges.

You were born-again to be led by the Holy Spirit; the purpose of the indwelling Spirit is for the leading of the Spirit. You are not just the habitation of the Spirit but you are inhabited to be directed in a life of unlimited exploits. It is said of Jesus that He was led by the Spirit and He *'returned in the power of the Spirit into Galilee: and there went out a fame of him through all the region round about'* (Luke 4:14). When you are led by the Spirit, your notoriety will travel far as you tuck victory after victory under your belt; it will make you a wonder in the world not because of what you did but because of what He did *through* you. We must not be head-led believers but Spirit-led believers. Head-led believers will be like head-less chickens, running all over the place, bleeding and eventually dropping dead.

As a believer, it is important that you be led inwardly and not externally. You are to be led by the Spirit who is dwelling in you and on the inside, bearing witness with your spirit:

For as many as are led by the Spirit of God, they are the sons of God.

ROMANS 8:14

Know ye not that ye are the temple of God, and that the Spirit of God dwelleth in you?

1 CORINTHIANS 3:16

The Spirit itself beareth witness with our spirit, that we are the children of God:

ROMANS 8:16

The provoking of unlimited exploits become realities as you trust the leading of the Spirit on the inside of you. The way of exploits is not in the leaning on your natural understanding but on the leading of the Spirit's leading:

Trust in the Lord with all thine heart; and lean not unto thine own understanding. In all thy ways acknowledge him, and he shall direct thy paths. Be not wise in thine own eyes: fear the Lord, and depart from evil.

PROVERBS 3:5-7

You don't trust God with your head (or intellect) but with your heart (or spirit), where the indwelling Spirit of God bears witness. If you are not leaning on the leading of the Spirit then you will lean on the futility and vanity of the mind, as Paul shared, '*This I say therefore, and testify in the Lord, that ye henceforth walk not as other Gentiles walk, in the vanity of their mind, Having the understanding darkened, being alienated from the life of God through the ignorance that is in them, because of the blindness of their heart*' (Ephesians 4:17-18). As you follow the Spirit's leadings He enables the inaccessible to become accessible. Men and women who were impactful and influential in the Bible were those who knew the leadings of His Spirit; they heard the voice of the Lord. Once you hear the voice of the Lord then other voices do not matter.

The leading of the Spirit will make you a wonder in the world because of what He does through you

---

◔ King David

David knew the leading of the Spirit was crucial to success upon the earth. This is why his plea was, *'Take not thy Holy Spirit from me'* (Psalm 51:11) and *'The Lord is my shepherd; I shall not want. He maketh me to lie down in green pastures: he leadeth me beside the still waters'* (Psalm 23:1-2). Soon after David was anointed King over all of Israel, he had two encounters with the Philistines:

> *But when the Philistines heard that they had anointed David king over Israel, all the Philistines came up to seek David; and David heard of it, and went down to the hold. The Philistines also came and spread themselves in the valley of Rephaim. And David enquired of the Lord, saying, Shall I go up to the Philistines? wilt thou deliver them into mine hand? And the Lord said unto David, Go up: for I will doubtless deliver the Philistines into thine hand. And David came to Baalperazim, and David smote them there, and said, The Lord hath broken forth upon mine enemies before me, as the breach of waters. Therefore he called the name of that place Baalperazim. And there they left their images, and David and his men burned them. And the Philistines came up yet again, and spread themselves in the valley of Rephaim. And when David enquired of the Lord, he said, Thou shalt not go up; but fetch a compass behind them, and come upon them over against the mulberry trees. And let it be, when thou hearest the sound of a going in the tops of the mulberry trees, that then thou shalt bestir thyself: for then shall the Lord go out before thee, to smite the host of the Philistines. And David did so, as the Lord had commanded him; and smote the Philistines from Geba until thou come to Gazer.*
>
> 2 Samuel 5:17-25

The Philistines came to test the resolve of David. When David heard of their plan, he did not say, 'Let me test my army against the Philistines. We defeated them before and we can do so again.' No! The Scriptures said: 'David enquired of the Lord.' He made the prayer of enquiries.

You do not qualify for answers if you do not ask questions. David made his move only after he heard from the mouth of God. Notice these words:

❖ David enquired.
❖ The Lord said.
❖ David did so.

Being led by God is the privilege and right of every believer

---

Twice they came up against him and twice he went before God for his leading. Even after the first victory, David did not assume that because God answered before that the same agenda was on for the next battle. Again, David went back to God for his leading. Presumption triggers destruction. What was the end result for David when he obeyed the leading of the Lord? He experienced breakthrough and exploits. You see the word *Baalperazim* means *Lord of the breakthrough* and to put it in the words of David himself, 'The Lord has broken forth upon my enemies before as the breach of waters.' The leading of the Spirit is the cause for many exploits and breakthroughs.

Presumption triggers destruction

❧ Israel

One of the greatest lessons we learned from the Old Testament is how God led Israel through Moses out of captivity and guided them through the wilderness and the desert without being harmed:

*For the Lord's portion is his people; Jacob is the lot of his inheritance. He found him in a desert land, and in the waste howling wilderness; **he led him about, he instructed him,** he kept him as the apple of his eye. As an eagle stirreth up her nest, fluttereth over her young, spreadeth abroad her wings, taketh them, beareth them on her wings: **So the Lord alone did lead him,** and there was no strange god with him.*

He made him ride on the high places of the earth, that he might eat the increase of the fields; and he made him to suck honey out of the rock, and oil out of the flinty rock; Butter of kine, and milk of sheep, with fat of lambs, and rams of the breed of Bashan, and goats, with the fat of kidneys of wheat; and thou didst drink the pure blood of the grape.

DEUTERONOMY 32:9-14

Look at the sequence that took place when Israel allowed himself to be led of God alone:

❖ Found him in the desert and waste howling wilderness.

❖ Led him and instructed him.

❖ The Lord alone did lead him.

❖ Kept him as the apple of his eyes.

❖ Bore them on his wings.

❖ Made him to ride upon the high places.

❖ Eat of the increase of the fields.

❖ Made him to suck honey out of the rock and oil out of the flinty rock.

❖ Butter of kine, and milk of sheep, with fat of lambs, and rams of the breed of Bashan, and goats, with the fat of kidneys of wheat; and thou didst drink the pure blood of the grape.

We know that Israel did not move unless the pillar of cloud and the pillar of fire moved and went ahead of them, '*The Lord thy God, he will go over before thee, and he will destroy these nations from before thee, and thou shalt possess them: and Joshua, he shall go over before thee, as the Lord hath said*' (Deuteronomy 31:3). When God goes before you, He is leading you. This is what we mean by being led by the Spirit. Notice when God goes ahead of Israel their enemies are destroyed and Israel experiences great exploits. In our above Scripture reference, we are told that God found Jacob (meaning Israel) in a desert land and waste howling wilderness. Many times that is where we find ourselves, for one reason or another; we find ourselves in a desert and waste howling wilderness where nothing is growing and we experience barrenness and leanness. To break out of it we have to seek for the leading of God, otherwise we will waste away in the wilderness. When God found Israel in the desert and waste howling wilderness, it was a place of death and danger:

> *Who **led thee through that great and terrible wilderness, wherein were fiery serpents, and scorpions, and drought,** where there was no water; who brought thee forth water out of the rock of flint; Who fed thee in the wilderness with manna, which thy fathers knew not, that he might humble thee, and that he might prove thee, to do thee good at thy latter end;*
>
> DEUTERONOMY 8:15-16

In the wilderness there were fiery serpents and scorpions ready to strike, but God kept them safe as long as He led them. The fiery serpents and scorpions are a picture and types of demons who are ever ready to strike us when we are not led of God. Not only did God protect them from the serpents and other elements of the desert, He fed them with manna. When we are led we will be fed and never be thirsty again. There is a powerful statement in the book of Isaiah that will do us good to heed:

> ***And they thirsted not when he led them through the deserts:*** *he caused the waters to flow out of the rock for them: he clave the rock also, and the waters gushed out.*
>
> ISAIAH 48:21

When we are led we will be fed

ℰ Pillar of cloud and pillar of fire

The pillar of cloud by day and the pillar of fire by night were for the training of the people of God to constantly follow the leadings of God. The day and night pillars led and guided the Israelites during their exodus from Egyptian bondage, enabling them to travel safely and in the timing of God. This is an important point: when we are led by the Spirit, there is a synchronization between us, the plan of God and the timing of God which triggers exploits. We don't want to miss the timing of God and this is why we must follow the pillars by day and night. Moses explains this phenomenon for us:

> *And the Lord went before them by day in a pillar of a cloud, to lead them* *the way; and by night in a pillar of fire, to give them light; to go by day* *and night: He took not away the pillar of the cloud by day, nor the pillar* *of fire by night, from before the people.*
>
> EXODUS 13:21-22

> *Moreover thou leddest them in the day by a cloudy pillar; and in the night* *by a pillar of fire, to give them light in the way wherein they should go.*
>
> NEHEMIAH 9:12

They were to constantly watch the pillars for their movements. When the pillars moved, they moved and when the pillars stopped, they stopped. You see, the pillar of cloud by day and the pillar of fire by night were a type of the Holy Spirit's guidance and covering. The pillars were not just for guidance but for covering protection and a place of favor with God:

> *He spread a cloud for a covering; and fire to give light in the night.*
>
> PSALM 105:39

> *And it came to pass, that in the morning watch the Lord looked unto* *the host of the Egyptians through the pillar of fire and of the cloud, and* *troubled the host of the Egyptians, And took off their chariot wheels,* *that they drave them heavily: so that the Egyptians said, Let us flee from* *the face of Israel; for the Lord fighteth for them against the Egyptians.*
>
> EXODUS 14:24-25

When the pillars of cloud and fire moved to the back of Israel they protected them from being penetrated and invaded by the Egyptians. In addition to that, God troubled the Egyptian army and took off their chariot wheels. That is a supernatural exploit! You know that was a hard ride. The Egyptians fled from Israel because they knew God was fighting for Israel.

When we are led by the Spirit, there is a synchronization between us, the plan of God and the timing of God, which triggers exploits

---

ℰ Conquest of Jericho

Jericho was a stronghold. It was shut up with nobody going in and nobody coming out. After Joshua succeeded Moses, his first major assignment was to take Jericho. Previously, many others had tried, only to fail miserably. You can understand the thoughts going through the mind of Joshua. As Joshua was in meditation and prayer, something unusual happened:

> *And it came to pass, when Joshua was by Jericho, that he lifted up his eyes and looked, and, behold, there stood a man over against him with his sword drawn in his hand: and Joshua went unto him, and said unto him, Art thou for us, or for our adversaries? And he said, Nay; but as captain of the host of the Lord am I now come. And Joshua fell on his face to the earth, and did worship, and said unto him, What saith my lord unto his servant?*
>
> JOSHUA 5:13-14

To conquer Jericho, Joshua needed the Lord to go ahead of him as the Captain of the host. God is the commander in chief, the general and the captain that went before Joshua and gave him a supernatural exploit that had not been done before. Whenever we let God go before us, He fights our battles. Joshua did not even need to fight. After receiving his instructions, he led Israel on a march around Jericho. Can you imagine the stupefying look on the face of their enemies who watched them march for seven days, blowing the trumpet?

You can hear the mockery of the people, 'I thought they came to take over our city. I guess it's just a free concert we are getting.' Their walking around did not make sense but they sure got their exploits: the ground opened up and the mega walls of Jericho sunk through. The leading of the Spirit will cause the walls of obstruction opposing you to cause your Jericho to sink into the ground so you can get to your destination.

☙ Exploits of Samson

The exploits of Samson were due to the Spirit of God, '*And the woman bare a son, and called his name Samson: and the child grew, and the Lord blessed him. And the Spirit of the Lord began to move him at times in the camp of Dan between Zorah and Eshtaol*' (Judges 13:24-25). Samson could tear a lion into pieces, lift up gates, destroy ropes with which he was bound and destroy the enemies of Israel, because of the leading of the Spirit. Over and over in the Bible you will see this term, '*The Spirit of the Lord came upon...*' It was so in the lives of David, Elijah and Samson, to name but a few. Every time this was the case, supernatural exploits were done. Therefore, any time the Spirit of God comes upon someone, there will be exploits. I want to draw your attention to an interesting event that took place in the life of Samson:

> And when he came unto Lehi, **the Philistines shouted against him:** *and* **the Spirit of the Lord came mightily upon him,** *and the cords that were upon his arms became as flax that was burnt with fire, and his bands loosed from off his hands.* **And he found a new jawbone of an ass, and put forth his hand, and took it, and slew a thousand men therewith.** *And Samson said, With the jawbone of an ass, heaps upon heaps, with the jaw of an ass have I slain a thousand men.*
>
> JUDGES 15:14-16

The Philistines shouted against Samson and the Spirit of God rose up in him and he shouted them down by slaying them. That was a shout which they regretted. Don't ever let the devil shout at you and you just sit there and take it. No! No! No! The same Holy Spirit moving upon Samson's life is now resident in you. Samson slew one thousand Philistines. You can be sure that was not what the Philistines were bargaining for. The Spirit of God will give you the last shout over the devil.

Today, the believer has the dual working of the Holy Spirit: the Spirit *within* and the Spirit *upon*. He is residing within us and leading, in order to come upon and do exploits. The question remains, 'How am I led by the Spirit?'

CHAPTER 15
SEVEN WAYS TO IDENTIFY
THE LEADINGS OF THE SPIRIT

IN closing this book, I want to give you simple keys to help you to tap into the leading of the Spirit. First of all, as I stated previously, being led by God is the believer's right and privilege. God is unwavering in His commitment to leading you:

> *Thus saith the Lord, thy Redeemer, the Holy One of Israel; I am the Lord thy God which teacheth thee to profit, **which leadeth thee by the way that thou shouldest go.***
>
> ISAIAH 48:17

> *I will instruct thee and teach thee in the way which thou shalt go: I will guide thee with mine eye.*
>
> PSALM 32:8

> *He that hath an ear, let him hear what the Spirit saith unto the churches*
>
> REVELATION 2:7

Secondly, when you are led by the Spirit, it is a proof that you are maturing in God as a son. Paul said, '*As many as are led by the Spirit of God, they are the sons of God*' (Romans 8:14). The Greek word for *son* is *huios*, meaning matured son.

There are many ways that the Spirit of God can and will lead us but the predominant ways that He will lead us are through:

❖ The guidance of His Word.
❖ The witness of the Spirit.

❧ The Word and the Witness

It is obvious that the number one way that God will guide us is through His Word. He guides us from and through His Word. I have written much about it in my other books and volumes have been written on the subject. In this book we will mainly focus on the leading of the Spirit. The voice of His Word is for the general will of God for our lives but the voice of the Spirit is for the specific will of God for our lives. Many times we miss the guidance or voice of the Holy Spirit because we are looking for the spectacular and the sensational. We are looking for an angel to appear, hearing the audible voice of God, a dream, a heavenly vision or a trance. These things may happen if God so chooses but you need to realize that the predominant way the Spirit leads the believer is through the inward witness of the Spirit.

Some have called the inward witness – as it pertains to guidance – such things as *a knowing, an impression, perception, an inner prompting, an inner voice, something told me, a hunch, a still small voice, an intuition, a premonition, a restlessness within, peace or lack or peace* and *an inward voice*. I can tell you from experience that sometimes that inward voice in my Spirit sounded like the audible voice of God. Even though I did not hear it with my physical ears, it resounded loud and clear within my being. Stop looking for the sensational. If it happens thank God for it but look to the inward leading and inward witness of the Spirit. You need to see that the inward witness is just as supernatural as guidance through visions or the appearance of an angel; it is just not as spectacular. Oswald Chambers made this statement many years ago, '*The voice of the Spirit of God is as gentle as a summer breeze – so gentle that unless you are living in complete fellowship and oneness with God, you will never hear it.*'

The inward witness is just as supernatural as guidance through visions, the audible voice of God or the appearance of an angel; it is just not as spectacular

---

In your quest to be led by the Spirit you need to be ever conscious of these pivotal verses from Romans, Corinthians, Galatians and John. If I was you, I would meditate upon these verses until they go through your spirit, soul and body:

*For as many as are led by the Spirit of God, they are the sons of God. For ye have not received the spirit of bondage again to fear; but ye have received the Spirit of adoption, whereby we cry, Abba, Father. **The Spirit itself beareth witness with our spirit, that we are the children of God:***

ROMANS 8:14-16

I say the truth in Christ, I lie not, my conscience also bearing me witness in the Holy Ghost.

ROMANS 9:1

*And because ye are sons, **God hath sent forth the Spirit of his Son into your hearts, crying,** Abba, Father.*

GALATIANS 4:6

*Now we have received, not the spirit of the world, but the spirit which is of God; that we might know the things that are freely given to us of God. Which things also we speak, not in the words which man's wisdom teacheth, but which the Holy Ghost teacheth; **comparing spiritual things with spiritual.** But the natural man receiveth not the things of the Spirit of God: for they are foolishness unto him: **neither can he know them, because they are spiritually discerned.***

1 CORINTHIANS 2:12-14

But ye have an unction from the Holy One, and ye know all things.

1 JOHN 2:20

But the anointing which ye have received of him abideth in you, and ye need not that any man teach you: but as the same anointing teacheth you of all things, and is truth, and is no lie, and even as it hath taught you, ye shall abide in him.

1 JOHN 2:27

*And there are three that **bear witness in earth**, the Spirit, and the water, and the blood: and these three agree in one. If we receive the witness of men, **the witness of God is greater**: for this is the witness of God which he hath testified of his Son.*

1 John 5:8-9

He that believeth on the Son of God hath the witness in himself.

1 John 5:10

The Lord is not dumb in the midst of His family, though, alas, some of His children appear to be dull of hearing. Though the Urim and Thummim are no longer to be seen upon the breasts of mortal men, yet the oracle is not silent. O that we were always ready to hear the loving voice of the Lord – Charles Haddon Spurgeon

---

The leading of the Spirit is mainly done by the Holy Spirit bearing witness with our spirit. Paul emphatically said, '*As many as are led by THE SPIRIT OF GOD, they are the sons of God.*' Most people do not realize that the last few chapters of the Gospel of John – namely from chapters 13-17 – are the last 24-hours of Jesus' life before He was crucified. **Jay Smith – The Ultimate Bible Summary Collection** has this to say about the following chapters:

The events in Chapters 13-17 occur less than 24 hours before Jesus' death. They describe the details of the Last Supper with Jesus and His disciples. **Jesus taught many important topics to the Disciples during this time. Some of these were topics about the Kingdom, and about the work of the Holy Spirit that would be sent to them.** He also prays for Himself, His disciples, and for all the future believers.

Jay Smith
The Ultimate Bible Summary Collection

Prior to His death, Jesus explicitly told the disciples of the ministry of the Holy Spirit. Before someone dies, they pass on their most important advice to their loved ones. Last words matter and Jesus passed on the most important advice to His disciples about the ministry of the Holy Spirit before He faced death:

*Howbeit when he, the Spirit of truth, is come, **he will guide you** into all truth: for he shall not speak of himself; but whatsoever he shall hear, that shall he speak: and **he will shew you things to come**. He shall glorify me: for he shall receive of mine, and **shall shew it unto you**.*

JOHN 16:13-14

*But when the Comforter is come, whom I will send unto you from the Father, even the Spirit of truth, which proceedeth from the Father, he shall **testify** of me.*

JOHN 15:26

The Holy Spirit leads by the inward witness that testifies within you. He is a testifier: someone who gives evidence as a witness. A witness is someone who confirms, substantiates and verifies the testimony of another; he confirms whether what is being presented is true or untrue. The Holy Spirit helps us in our walk with God by confirming and resonating something in our spirit as a witness that gives us a green light. This is how He leads us through our spirit. The book of Romans did not say, 'As many as are led by prophets or apostles.' You need to get this: the Holy Spirit is directly responsible to lead you, to guide you and to show you things to come. He leads you directly today. Therefore do not seek prophets and apostles for guidance; they do not lead us but can only confirm or encourage us in the direction that God has already shown to us.

A witness is someone who confirms, substantiates
and verifies the testimony of another

Allow me to reiterate this point again: the chief way the New Testament believer receives guidance is through the leading of the Spirit by the *inward witness*. The Holy Spirit drops something into your spirit. It is a joint witness in your spirit. There is a stamp of approval on the inside. Something resonates in your inner being. This is a Spirit-to-spirit transaction.

Not only was Jesus led of the Spirit but we also see the leadings of the Spirit in the early church through the book of Acts. I went through my online Bible and searched for the words *spirit* and *Holy Ghost* within the book of Acts and these are some examples of the leadings and the witnessing of the Spirit:

*Then the **Spirit said** unto Philip, Go near, and join thyself to this chariot.*
ACTS 8:29

*While Peter thought on the vision, the **Spirit said** unto him, Behold, three men seek thee.*
ACTS 10:19

*And the **Spirit bade** me go with them, nothing doubting. Moreover these six brethren accompanied me, and we entered into the man's house:*
ACTS 11:12

*And there stood up one of them named Agabus, and **signified by the Spirit** that there should be great dearth throughout all the world: which came to pass in the days of Claudius Cæsar.*
ACTS 11:28

*As they ministered to the Lord, and fasted, **the Holy Ghost said**, Separate me Barnabas and Saul for the work whereunto I have called them.*
ACTS 13:2

*So they, being **sent forth by the Holy Ghost**, departed unto Seleucia; and from thence they sailed to Cyprus.*
ACTS 13:4

*For **it seemed good to the Holy Ghost**, and to us, to lay upon you no greater burden than these necessary things.*

ACTS 15:28

*Now when they had gone throughout Phrygia and the region of Galatia, and were **forbidden of the Holy Ghost** to preach the word in Asia.*

ACTS 16:6

*After they were come to Mysia, they assayed to go into Bithynia: but **the Spirit suffered them not**.*

ACTS 16:7

*Save that the **Holy Ghost witnesseth** in every city, saying that bonds and afflictions abide me.*

ACTS 20:23

*And finding disciples, we tarried there seven days: who said to Paul **through the Spirit**, that he should not go up to Jerusalem.*

ACTS 21:4

The voice of His Word is for the general will of God for our lives but the voice of His Spirit is for the specific will of God for our lives

---

It is clear to us that the Spirit of God communicates to the church. In fact Paul said, '*Now the Spirit speaketh expressly...*' (1 Timothy 4:1). He is the master communicator and He wants to communicate to you through your spirit. He speaks, He leads, He prompts, He forbids, He bids, He guides and He moves or nudges. As I mentioned earlier on, some have called it premonition, intuition, perception, a hunch, a check in my spirit, an uneasiness, a restlessness, a knowing, still small voice or an inward voice. All of these take place in your inward man. It is important to be aware of these when making decisions. Life is full of decisions and choices and we have to make the right ones. When you make a choice, you have set yourself on a course and every course has consequences; there is just no way around this fact. This is why we must be led by the Spirit. In my experience I have discovered the witness of the Spirit comes in seven expressions. Others may add to this list but these seven are fundamental. They are somewhat similar and overlap but through experience, as you seek the leading of the Spirit, you will be acquainted with them and it really would not matter how you label them, other than *being led by the Spirit*. They are not in order of importance:

* Scripture quickening.
* The witness bearing of the Spirit to your spirit.
* Inner promptings.
* Peace and joy, or lack of it and restlessness.
* Perception.
* Check your inward *seemer*: 'It *seemed* good to Holy Spirit and to us.'
* Inward voice.

> *When you make a choice, you have set yourself on a course and when you are on a course there will be consequences. There is just no way around this fact and this is why you need to be led by the Spirit*

> Scripture quickening

The more you get into the Word and know the Word, the easier it is for you to be led by the Holy Spirit. Meditation is key for quickened direction. God specifically told Joshua as he embarked on a new journey:

This book of the law shall not depart out of thy mouth; but thou shalt meditate therein day and night, that thou mayest observe to do according to all that is written therein: for then thou shalt make thy way prosperous, and then thou shalt have good success.

JOSHUA 1:8

Meditation means not just thinking the Word but speaking the Word also. The more you speak the Word, the more the Word will eventually speak back to you. I'm sure it has happened to many believers who are loaded up on the Word daily and when they encounter a problem, all of a sudden a Scripture pops out of nowhere and into their mind. That is the Holy Spirit leading – through a quickened Word. When you experience this, don't overrule it as just something that popped into your mind: this is the Holy Spirit's leading, pulling a Scripture that you have premeditated upon and making it alive, with the answer to your particular situation. When this happens you have just tapped into the *rhema* of God: the quickened, living word that is a sword, cutting through the situation.

Meditation is key for quickened direction

> The witness bearing of the Spirit to your spirit

Paul said, '*The Spirit itself beareth witness with our spirit, that we are the children of God*' (Romans 8:16). How do you know that you are a child of God? There is no born-again birth certificate. Your church may have given you a certificate when you were baptized in water but there is no outward paper evidence that you are a child of God except that the Holy Spirit bears witness with your spirit. Something resonates in your spirit, giving you spiritual confidence and understanding. You just have an inner assurance – an inward knowing – because of the inward communication of the Holy Spirit. To *resonate* means to relate harmoniously and to strike a chord. It is the confirmed evidence of the Holy Spirit to your spirit. The apostle John revealed the witness-bearing of the Spirit this way, '*But ye have an unction from the Holy One, and ye know all things*' (1 John 2:20). How do you know all things? By the *unction* in you! John was warning the believers of seducers who would endeavor to seduce them into denying Christ.

How can we tell what is right and what is wrong?

John expounds further:

These things have I written unto you concerning them that seduce you. But the anointing which ye have received of him abideth in you, and ye need not that any man teach you: but as the same anointing teacheth you of all things, and is truth, and is no lie, and even as it hath taught you, ye shall abide in him.

1 JOHN 2:26-27

What John was drilling into the believers was to trust the indwelling unction or the indwelling anointing, who teaches us and has been teaching from the day of our salvation. That indwelling unction and anointing is the Holy Spirit. Sometimes you hear things and something inside just does not resonate with what you are hearing. That's the anointing within you, teaching and keeping you safe. Your head may be clueless but inside there's a *knowing*. Sometimes you can't even explain it but you just know something is off. This has happened to me many times.

The leading of the Spirit is mainly done by the Holy Spirit bearing witness with our spirit

---

I remember, years ago, people and Christian television were raving about a certain minister being a great revivalist and the next move of God. I had never heard or seen the man prior to this. So one day, I was visiting someone in England and that particular minister was on television. My host was busy telling me how great this person was. I listened for a few minutes and it was like putting oil in a glass of water: it does not mix. My spirit did not resonate with what I saw or heard on television. Some of what he was saying sounded like it was OK but inside me there were alarm bells going off. I did not say anything to my host but later I told my wife, 'There is something not right about this guy.' Some time later, a lot of stuff came out about him and his doctrine which were off target completely.

What was the discomfort within me towards this situation? It was the witness-bearing of the Spirit, safeguarding my life and He will do so in many other instances.

Whenever you make decisions – and whatever they may be – watch out for the joint confirmation, the joint witness of the Holy Spirit with your spirit. Look at these verses again:

For as many as are led by the Spirit of God, they are the sons of God. For ye have not received the spirit of bondage again to fear; but ye have received the Spirit of adoption, whereby we cry, Abba, Father. **The Spirit itself beareth witness with our spirit, that we are the children of God:**

ROMANS 8:14-16

And because ye are sons, **God hath sent forth the Spirit of his Son into your hearts, crying,** *Abba, Father.*

GALATIANS 4:6

Now we have received, not the spirit of the world, but the spirit which is of God; that we might know the things that are freely given to us of God. Which things also we speak, not in the words which man's wisdom teacheth, but which the Holy Ghost teacheth; **comparing spiritual things with spiritual.** *But the natural man receiveth not the things of the Spirit of God: for they are foolishness unto him:* **neither can he know them, because they are spiritually discerned.**

1 CORINTHIANS 2:12-14

But ye have an unction from the Holy One, and ye know all things.

1 JOHN 2:20

But the anointing which ye have received of him abideth in you, and ye need not that any man teach you: but as the same anointing teacheth you of all things, and is truth, and is no lie, and even as it hath taught you, ye shall abide in him.

1 JOHN 2:27

*And there are three **that bear witness in earth**, the Spirit, and the water,
and the blood: and these three agree in one. If we receive the witness of
men, **the witness of God is greater**: for this is the witness of God which
he hath testified of his Son.*

1 John 5:8-9

Look at this phrase, '*Comparing spiritual things with spiritual... the natural
man receiveth not the things of the Spirit of God: for they are foolishness
unto him: neither can he know them, because they are spiritually discerned.*'
The Holy Spirit, who searches all things and knows all things, informs your
spirit man of spiritual things and as you compare them with what you are
hearing or being presented with from someone, if the comparison does not
match what you have in your spirit you should walk away from it. I also
want to draw your attention to a verse in the epistle of John:

*And there are three that **bear witness in earth**, the Spirit, and the water,
and the blood: and these three agree in one. If we receive the witness of
men, **the witness of God is greater**: for this is the witness of God which
he hath testified of his Son.*

1 John 5:8-9

*He that believeth on the Son of God hath the **witness** in himself:*

1 John 5:10

From the day you became born-again, the Spirit of God has been bearing
witness in you, regarding your salvation and sonship. He will also use the
same method of witness-bearing to guide you in all other affairs of your
life. Before we move on to the next aspect I want to bring to your attention
this verse in John's epistle, '*And there are three that **bear witness in earth**,
the Spirit, and the water, and the blood: and these three agree in one.*' Over
the years there has been a lot of criticism saying this verse should not be
in the Bible. I am not going to get into that discussion but I just want you
to notice the words, 'three bear witness in the earth'. Again we see the term

'bear witness' that correspond with what Paul said. John said, '*there are three that bear witness in earth, the Spirit, the water and the blood.*' Again there is much contention as to what the three witnesses are. In my studying, the three witnesses refer to the Holy Spirit, the water (which is the Word – Ephesians 5:26) and the blood (which is the Cross of Calvary). In other words, everything that is right will align with the work of Jesus on the Cross, with the Scriptures and with the Holy Spirit. Anything that deviates from these three is not of God.

The chief way the New Testament believer receives guidance is through the leading of the Spirit by the inward witness

---

> Inner promptings

An inner prompting is a little voice, or a knowing that you have in your spirit while everything in the natural seems fine. Your mind might even be telling you everything looks OK and yet something on the inside is not sitting well. It is like the two sides of the magnet that do not connect. Most of the time, inner promptings manifest as, 'Something tells me...', 'this little voice inside me' and 'I just keep getting this impression'. Many times we ignore these promptings – to our detriment. Look what Paul says:

> *And when Silas and Timotheus were come from Macedonia, Paul was pressed in the spirit, and testified to the Jews that Jesus was Christ.*
> ACTS 18:5

This is a spiritual impression. It is not a physical sensation but something down in your inners: you feel impressed about something or someone. Some have called this prompting a *gut feeling* or a premonition. A prompting can also be the receiving of ideas, concepts, images and thoughts into your spirit man that you know are not from your imaginations. These are from the Holy Spirit, making a deposit into your spirit. Follow that leading and there will be exploits.

❭ Peace and joy, or lack of peace and restlessness

This is such an important aspect of the guidance of the Holy Spirit and yet millions of believers override this phenomenon constantly. The reason we do so is because we do not see it as the leading and guidance of the Spirit due to its simplicity: it is not sensational or spectacular enough. Yet as a believer this is one of the most verifiable ways the Spirit leads us on a regular basis in our daily lives. As an example, sometimes the moment you meet someone, a check or buzzer goes off in your spirit. You may be smiling at the person, shaking hands and everything looks fine but there is a check in your spirit. There is no peace to move forward with that person. A restlessness is going on in your spirit. As another example, you could be presented with a business deal that, even though your head is somewhat perplexed about it, there is a peace on the inside.

And let the peace of God rule in your hearts...
COLOSSIANS 3:15

For ye shall go out with joy, and be led forth with peace: the mountains and the hills shall break forth before you into singing, and all the trees of the field shall clap their hands.
ISAIAH 55:12

Let us therefore follow after the things which make for peace...
ROMANS 14:19

Follow peace with all men...
HEBREWS 12:14

When you feel a sense of restlessness in your spirit, do not override it and move on with what you were going to do: stop and pray it through in the spirit until you know what to do. Restlessness is an indication to seek God and not to make a sudden move. If you have peace, move with it; if you don't have peace, don't move. At times we have called it the green light or the red light. If it's the green light, we move on but if it is a red light we stop.

> Perception

Two vivid examples of people who walked in perception in the New Testament were the Lord Jesus and the apostle Paul. Because they walked in perception they could avoid deception and destruction. You can see that in the earthly ministry of Jesus. We see the value of divine guidance through perception in Acts 27, when Paul could have lost his life but instead saved his own life and the lives of the men with him in the ship. That event in the book of Acts was put there for us to see the importance of the inward witness of the Spirit through perception:

And when it was determined that we should sail into Italy, they delivered Paul and certain other prisoners unto one named Julius, a centurion of Augustus' band. And entering into a ship of Adramyttium, we launched, meaning to sail by the coasts of Asia; one Aristarchus, a Macedonian of Thessalonica, being with us. And the next day we touched at Sidon. And Julius courteously entreated Paul, and gave him liberty to go unto his friends to refresh himself. And when we had launched from thence, we sailed under Cyprus, because the winds were contrary. And when we had sailed over the sea of Cilicia and Pamphylia, we came to Myra, a city of Lycia. And there the centurion found a ship of Alexandria sailing into Italy; and he put us therein. And when we had sailed slowly many days, and scarce were come over against Cnidus, the wind not suffering us, we sailed under Crete, over against Salmone; And, hardly passing it, came unto a place which is called The fair havens; nigh whereunto was the city of Lasea.

Now when much time was spent, and when sailing was now dangerous, because the fast was now already past, **Paul admonished them, And said unto them, Sirs, I perceive that this voyage will be with hurt and much damage, not only of the lading and ship, but also of our lives. Nevertheless the centurion believed the master and the owner of the ship, more than those things which were spoken by Paul. And because** *the haven was not commodious to winter in, the more part advised to depart thence also, if by any means they might attain to Phenice, and there to winter; which is an haven of Crete, and lieth toward the south west and north west. And when the south wind blew softly, supposing that they had obtained their purpose, loosing thence, they sailed close by Crete. But not long after there arose against it a tempestuous wind, called Euroclydon. And when the ship was caught, and could not bear up into the wind, we let her drive. And running under a certain island which is called Clauda, we had much work to come by the boat:*

ACTS 27:1-16

While the professionals trusted in their expertise, Paul trusted the inward perception of the Holy Spirit. When he told them, '*Sirs, I perceive that this voyage will be with hurt and much damage, not only of the lading and ship, but also of our lives*', they did not believe him; they just assumed it was a cockamamie excuse not to be brought before Caesar. Besides, the weather looked good and everything in the natural seemed fine. The weather man did not say there was a storm over the horizon. However this little Holy Ghost man knew things in his spirit that they were not privy to. He had the perception of the Spirit of God. Some call that an intuition. They overruled his perception and it almost cost them their lives. If it were not for that little man, they would be the feeding frenzy of predatory fish in the Mediterranean sea.

Pay attention to these words, '*And when the ship was caught, and could not bear up into the wind, we let her drive. And running under a certain island which is called Clauda, we had much work to come by the boat.*' This is what happens when we override perception or inward witness of the Spirit: we get caught and we are no longer in control of the ship of our lives. The word *perceive* – as employed by Paul – is *theoreo* in Greek, meaning to discern, identify and detect. It means *to perceive with the inner man* and it also means God spoke. Job tells us, '*For God speaketh once, yea twice, yet man perceiveth it not*' (Job 33:14). Perception picks up on the voice of God. Pay attention to the perceptions, intuitions, impressions and the checks in your spirit. Sometimes you can't explain them but it's just that you sense something on the inside. That's the Holy Spirit.

> Check your inward *seemer*: 'It seemed good to the Holy Ghost and to us'

Here is another way of the witness bearing of the Spirit. We find this reality in the book of Acts:

For it seemed good to the Holy Ghost, and to us...

ACTS 15:28

For it was the will of The Spirit of Holiness and also of us...
ARAMAIC BIBLE IN PLAIN ENGLISH

For it was the Holy Spirit's decision – and ours –
HOLMAN CHRISTIAN STANDARD BIBLE

The Holy Spirit and we have agreed
GOD'S WORD TRANSLATION

Notice 'it seemed good to the Holy Ghost and to us' is rendered as 'the decision of the Holy Spirit that we agreed with'. This can be experienced on a corporate or personal level. On a corporate level it is when someone says they have something from God, share it and others testify to its credibility. Most often, people would say, 'I have this witness in my spirit' meaning *I concur and have the same agreement in my spirit*. On a personal level we see this in the life of Silas, who decided to stay back in Antioch after he was sent there for a short mission trip:

Then pleased it the apostles and elders, *with the whole church, to send chosen men of their own company to Antioch with Paul and Barnabas; namely, Judas surnamed Barsabas, and Silas, chief men among the brethren... We have sent therefore Judas and Silas, who shall also tell you* *the same things by mouth. **For it seemed good to the Holy Ghost,** and to us, to lay upon you no greater burden than these necessary things... And Judas and Silas, being prophets also themselves, exhorted the brethren with many words, and confirmed them. And after they had tarried there a space, they were let go in peace from the brethren unto the apostles. Notwithstanding **it pleased Silas to abide there still.***

Acts 15:22-34

I have highlighted three sentences to get your attention to what was being said:

❖ Then pleased it the apostles and elders to send chosen men...
❖ For it seemed good to the Holy Ghost and to us...
❖ It pleased Silas to abide there still...

The words *pleased* and *seemed good* come from the same Greek word, *dokeo,* which means to think and in the context of the verses above mean 'to be beautiful'. We can write the verses this way:

❖ Then it was beautiful for the apostles and elders to send chosen men...
❖ For it was beautiful to the Holy Ghost and beautiful to us...
❖ It was beautiful for Silas to abide there still...

On both a corporate and personal level these were other examples of the leading and the witness of the Spirit. The apostles got it right to send Silas and Barnabas. Silas also got it right when he decided to stay. They were all following the leading of the Spirit. Have you ever wondered why Silas chose to stay there? He could have gone back with Judas. Somehow, when he was in Antioch, he had a beautiful witness, or velvety feeling on the inside of him that he should stay there. Is it coincidental that after Barnabas and Paul separated that Silas stepped in? No! God, who has foreknowledge, knew that Paul and Barnabas would separate. Through the leading of the Spirit – through following the *beautiful delight* in his spirit – Silas got the opportunity of a lifetime to be Paul's companion. 'Seemed good to us' and 'pleased Silas' were examples of the early church cooperating with the Holy Spirit's plans. You will also experience this in the days ahead of you; listen to the Holy Spirit to know where you should be.

I have received many invitations from different countries and I travel to many countries to minister, but there are some countries that no matter how often they invite me I have never been – and will not go because my *seemer* reacts negatively. At the time of writing this book in 2017 , I am preparing to go to Nigeria and that will be my 100th visit to that particular nation. Every time I think of Nigeria, my *seemer* is excited and it resonates well in my spirit. I am pleased to go there. Why? Because Nigeria is part of my call. There will be a joy, a beautiful inward sensation when you are in the place where God wants you to be.

Let me show you a powerful thing about the inward seemer. If I was to ask you this question, 'Who wrote the Bible?' No doubt – as Bible believers, because you believe in the inspiration and infallibility of the Scripture – you will say, 'God used men to write the Bible. It is divinely inspired.' And you are 100% right. Now let me ask you another question, 'Who wrote the Gospel of Luke and Acts of the Apostles?' If you have any Bible knowledge you will know it was Dr Luke. Well, why did Luke write them? Is it because he heard the audible voice of God or saw writing in the skies? No! See what Dr Luke said:

> *Forasmuch as many have taken in hand to set forth in order a declaration of those things which are most surely believed among us, Even as they delivered them unto us, which from the beginning were eyewitnesses, and ministers of the word; **It seemed good to me also**, having had perfect understanding of all things from the very first, to write unto thee in order, most excellent Theophilus, That thou mightest know the certainty of those things, wherein thou hast been instructed.*
>
> LUKE 1:1-4

Why did Luke write the Gospel of Luke? Because *'it seemed good to me.'* His Gospel went into the Canon of the Scripture not because he heard the audible voice of God but because he followed the inward witness, manifested through the *inward seemer*. What would have happened if Luke did not follow the *inward seemer*? We would be missing Luke's exposition of the humanity of Christ and the story of the early church, as well as the missionary journeys of the Apostle Paul. Our lives are richly blessed today because Luke followed his inward witness, the *inward seemer*.

〉 Inward voice

Many have described the inward voice as:

❖ The voice of conscience being the voice of your own spirit.

❖ The actual inward voice of the Holy Spirit. The actual inward voice of the Holy Spirit that comes with more authority when we hear it and it is not something to be disobeyed or disregarded.

〉 The voice of your spirit

The voice of conscience is the voice of your own spirit that will gnaw at you when you are making wrong decisions:

I say the truth in Christ, I lie not, my conscience also bearing me witness in the Holy Ghost

ROMANS 9:1

Your recreated spirit has a voice and it will speak to you. Paul referred to this inward voice of the inner man as the voice of conscience. It is that still, small voice that whispers to you. As a born-again believer, Paul had grasped the fact that he was a new creature with the Holy Spirit resident in him, making him the tabernacle of God. Therefore when his conscience alerted him, he understood that to be the voice of his spirit drawing from the Holy Spirit.

Here's a slight difference between the inward witness and the inward voice:

❖ The **inward witness** of the Spirit is the Holy Spirit bearing witness with your spirit.

❖ The **inward voice** – as it pertains to the conscience – is your spirit bearing witness with the Holy Spirit:

Beloved, if our heart condemn us not, then have we confidence toward God
1 JOHN 3:21

The heart condemning you is the voice of your conscience from your spirit. The Holy Spirit only convicts; He never condemns. However your own spirit man – through the conscience – *will* condemn you. When the heart does not condemn, it means there is a clean conscience, triggering confidence to proceed. The Holy Spirit guides us through a clean conscience. A guilty conscience is your spirit reacting to wrong doing and sin in your life:

I say the truth in Christ, I lie not, my conscience also bearing me witness in the Holy Ghost
ROMANS 9:1

And Paul, earnestly beholding the council, said, Men and brethren, I **have lived in all good conscience before God until this day.**
ACTS 23:1

And herein do I exercise myself, to have always a conscience void of offence toward God, and toward men.
ACTS 24:16

Your conscience will prick you when you are doing wrong and when you have done wrong. You can trust the conscience of the reborn spirit because it is linked to the Holy Spirit. Don't ever violate the voice of your conscience. Some have thought that simply because of disobedience and selfish pride they don't want to do what God the Holy Spirit is saying and others thought that the conscience is just natural, so turned a deaf ear to the gnawing voice within. When you overrule your conscience, you shut down the voice of your spirit and yield to the flesh and sin, which then blocks the voice of God in your life. Here are three impacting statements from Paul:

For our rejoicing is this, the testimony of our conscience, that in simplicity and godly sincerity, not with fleshly wisdom, but by the grace of God, we have had our conversation in the world, and more abundantly to you-ward.

2 CORINTHIANS 1:12

Holding faith, and a good conscience; which some having put away concerning faith have made shipwreck

1 TIMOTHY 1:19

I thank God, whom I serve from my forefathers with pure conscience, that without ceasing I have remembrance of thee in my prayers night and day;

2 TIMOTHY 1:3

When you overrule your conscience, you shut down the voice of your spirit and yield to the flesh and sin

---

A pure and clean conscience is priceless. When you put away your conscience, you are on the road to shipwreck. Your conscience is the voice of your spirit – bearing witness with the Holy Spirit – to keep you clean and pure. The maintaining of a clean conscience enables you to be continuously guided by the Holy Spirit.

Now lets go to the inward voice as the voice of the Holy spirit in our spirit man. Many times that can sound like the audible voice of God, except that it is only you who heard it on the inside.

The prince of preachers, Charles Spurgeon, said this many years ago, *'The voice of God is the secret voice, unheard by any other ear which our own ear, opened by the spirit of God, recognises with joy.'* Whenever that occurs you have to obey promptly or the consequences could be fatal.

Years ago when I was living in London, England, I was invited to minister in a church in the South of England, in the city of Gosport, which is just over an 80 miles drive. Rosanna and I set out with a couple of our friends. The guys were in the front and the ladies at the back. We were driving and chatting on the expressway when all of a sudden I heard in my spirit, 'You need to pray now!' I just blurted out, 'Hey we have not prayed, we need to pray now.' I just opened my mouth, prayed and pleaded the protective power of the blood of Jesus on our journey. No sooner had I said Amen, a huge semi trailer truck overtook us then came into our lane and for some unknown reason just braked in front of us. We were traveling at 70 miles per hour. The abrupt braking of the semi truck in front of us caused my friend to press the brake but we could see the truck fast-approaching and we were just about to go under the rear of that tractor-trailer – which had no rear under-ride guard (Mansfield bar). We would have been decapitated or had some serious head injuries but we were able to stop in time, just short of the rear of the truck. Thank God for the inward voice of the Holy Ghost.

It pays great dividends to be closely acquainted with the Holy Spirit; He leads us and guides us into all the truth. He is your guide to great exploits and victory. To make yourself more sensitive to his leading for unlimited exploits you need to:

> Saturate yourself in the Word daily.

There is just no way around this fact. Esteem the Word more than your necessary food, as Job informed us (Job 23:12). The more you get into the Word, the more it will get into you; the more you meditate upon the Word, the more it will speak back to you. Be voracious in your appetite for the Word!

⟩ Pray in the Spirit

Pure and simple! The more you pray in tongues the more you sensitize your spirit with the Holy Spirit. Pray in your heavenly language – tongues. As you keep praying in tongues, it is your spirit – by the Holy Spirit – that prays. Learn to pay attention to the images, concepts, ideas, impressions and thoughts that well up in you when you pray in tongues.

⟩ Be swift to be a doer of the Word

James said to be '*a doer of the Word and not hearers only, deceiving your own selves*' (James 1:22). Deceiving your own heart means you deny yourself the ability to function and be led from your spirit. The more you *do* the Word, the more you are exercising the functioning of your spirit man, which then has a domino effect of making your more sensitive to other leadings of the Spirit.

⟩ Walk in love

Don't let anyone or anything take you off of the love walk. Don't let bitterness, anger, strife, jealousy, fussing and fightings get into your spirit. These are spirit -blockers and spirit-lockers. Allowing these will be a stumbling block for you to hear the voice of the Holy Spirit. They will defile you and put your spirit man in lockdown mode. Constantly meditate upon 1 Corinthians 13, confessing these verses and let them dictate your daily steps.

⟩ Be committed to asking the Holy Spirit for guidance

Many times we do not receive guidance and directions simply because we do not ask. We endeavor to fix our own problems by our expertise and experiences. The answer you never received is due to the question you never asked. James said, '*Ye have not because ye ask not.*' (James 4:3). As long as you think that you can fix it yourself, the Holy Spirit will step back and let you get on with it, He will never push His will and way on you.

He is a gentleman. Therefore you have to make it your priority to ask Him for His leading and guidance. Learn to ask questions. This is a great tip we can learn from King David, who enquired from God when facing the Philistines, '*Shall I go up to the Philistines? wilt thou deliver them into mine hand? And the Lord said unto David, Go up.*' (2 Samuel 5:19). Too many people are looking for long-winded answers when they have never tapped into short answers from God. He speaks in short sentences, '*Arise get thee to Zarephath*' (1 Kings 17:9). So ask Him questions. Get used to asking Him questions and He will answer you.

> Don't overrule the inklings of your spirit

Whether it is an intuition, an inward knowing, your conscience, a lack of peace or a gut feeling, do not overrule and dismiss it. If you keep overruling and overriding these inner warnings and witnesses, after a while you will not pick up on them anymore due to constantly suffocating and stifling them. Pay attention to them. To constantly dismiss them is another way of quenching the Spirit (1 Thessalonians 5:19). Sometimes we have these grand ideas of what it means to quench the Spirit in respect to church services and flow but we don't realize that we quench Him daily when we ignore the inward witnesses. Acting upon them will show you whether you were in the spirit or if it was just you.

> Ask in the small stuff

Some people wait till they have a gigantic problem to ask for guidance from the Holy Spirit. It is difficult to receive direction and guidance for big issues when you have never received direction for small issues. Don't wait for a life and death situation to ask for direction: ask in the small, menial stuff as you get used to the voice and the leading of the Spirit. Here's a simple analogy to understand this: it is highly unlikely that you will be able to curl 50lbs dumbbells if you have not curled 10lbs dumbbells. Starting with the smaller weights sets you up for the heavier weights later and likewise, getting direction in the small issues sets you up for direction in the big issues later.

I started training myself years ago. For years I have traveled extensively and being picked up at airports is a normal event for me. Sometimes my ride would be late to pick me up so just to keep myself sharp I would ask the Holy Spirit, 'Is he coming from the left or right?' Or 'What color or make of the car would be?' Then I would listen inwardly. At the beginning I missed it many times but as time went by I began to be able to get it right. At the beginning when I missed the mark, it was no big deal and no one was hurt. So start with small stuff.

〉 Maintain an attitude of joy

Maintaining an attitude of praise, worship and joy is imperative to pick up on the voice of the Spirit. Look at the words of the book of Isaiah, '*Ye shall have a song, as in the night when a holy solemnity is kept; and gladness of heart, as when one goeth with a pipe to come into the mountain of the Lord, to the mighty One of Israel. And the Lord shall cause his glorious voice to be heard...*' (Isaiah 30:29-30). When will we hear the glorious voice of the Lord? When we have a song and gladness of heart! You see, an attitude of joy attracts the voice of God. The Psalmist wrote, '*I call to remembrance my song in the night: I commune with mine own heart: and my spirit made diligent search.*' (Psalm 77:6). Complaining, moaning, whining or murmuring indicate you are listening to yourself and searching through your problems but worship, praise and joy open you up to listen to God.

〉 Be quiet

Finally, in your quest to be led by the Spirit, you need to learn the art of silence. This is so hard for many people living in hectic cities and with a busy lifestyle, nonetheless it is imperative because if you are going through life's routines at 100 miles per hour daily you don't have time to sit and listen. You have to be quiet to listen. God has already said, '*For thus saith the Lord God, the Holy One of Israel; In returning and rest shall ye be saved; in quietness and in confidence shall be your strength: and ye would not.*' (Isaiah 30:15). Paul said, '*And that ye study to be quiet...*' (1 Thessalonians 4:11).

Learn the art and vocabulary of silence. Even Jesus had to withdraw Himself to a solitary place to pray and hear from God. If Jesus had to do it, so will you! Even if you have to wait late in the night or very early in the morning when everybody is still sleeping, the serene atmosphere will aid you to heed the voice of His Spirit or perceive the inward witness. The Scripture is clear, *'Be still and know that I am God...'* (Psalm 46:10).

You have been called to a life of great exploits but it takes:

❖ Knowing God.
❖ Being strong.
❖ Having imposing, aggressive faith.
❖ Being persistent in importunate prayer.
❖ Being led by the Holy Ghost.

Use the information that you have received and impact your destiny.

About the Author

Dr. Glenn Arekion is a uniquely gifted teacher and conference speaker. He conveys the Word of Truth in a simple, yet dynamic and motivational, way. With more than two decades' experience, he travels the globe mentoring leaders, equipping businessmen, and ministering to people, helping them to fulfill their purpose in life. He is a captivating and much sought-after speaker.

The author of thirty books, Glenn is dedicated to transforming lives from defeat into victory. His teaching materials are sold in many countries and are popular among those with a desire to grow strong in faith and experience great success.

Glenn is apostolic in his thrust of ministry. He believes in establishing churches, and teaching and training pastors in their calling. His television program, Faithlift, airs twice a week on The Word Network. Faithlift is also a daily television program on the Faithworld Channel in the U.K. and all over Europe.

Born in Mauritius, Africa, but raised and educated in London, Glenn holds a master's degree and three doctorate degrees.

Glenn and his beautiful wife, Rosanna, have three children – Lisa, Ethan, and Jodie – and reside in Kentucky.

Author Contact

Glenn Arekion Ministries
P.O. Box 197777
Louisville, KY 40259, USA
mail@glennarekion.org
www.glennarekion.org

People Like You... Make People Like Me... Go!

EVERY major ministry making an impact in the world today is blessed with faithful financial and prayerful partners. Partnership with a ministry is a crucial way for the Gospel to go in all the world. Together, I am totally convinced that we can impact the world and accomplish great things to the glory of God.

I have a simple vision burning in my spirit to unveil the Good News to sinners and saints that victory is available in life through Jesus Christ. Therefore **partners** are an important part of this ministry and their assistance enable us to accomplish the following:

❖ Globally preach the Gospel through the media: The Word Network;
❖ Travel and preach the Gospel to the nations;
❖ Author books anointed by the Holy Spirit, endowed with information that will radically transform the lives of believers;
❖ Healing crusades and conventions worldwide;
❖ Planting churches in different nations.

Partners help us to do what we cannot do by ourselves.

Not everyone is called to full time ministry but every one is called to reach our world. Everyone who actively participates in supporting Glenn Arekion Ministries with their finances and prayers will receive credit and rewards for whatever this ministry accomplishes.

So join me as a partner today and be part of this end-time harvest! Together, let's reach the millions who need to hear the gospel of Jesus Christ. Your partnership with me will give you the personal satisfaction of being part of a strong ministry that is doing its best to fulfill the Great Commission. You can have the confidence of sowing into a ministry of integrity, knowing that your support is accomplishing the work of the gospel.

Visit **glennarekion.org/partner** today and join us!

Further books by Dr Glenn Arekion...

Available online at glennarekion.org
Download eBooks and MP3 messages instantly

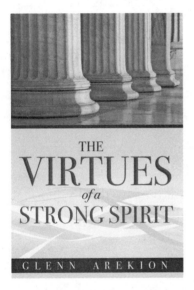

God created man with words of dominion and His original intent was for man to live from the inside out. This simply means to dominate the flesh from the spirit, and the natural from the spiritual. Since the fall of Adam, man has been living from his flesh, dominated by circumstances. Through the regeneration, our spirit man was reborn to win but the key is to know how to have a strong spirit. The stronger we are in our spirit the easier it will be for us to resist the attacks of the devil.

Living in the last days, it is imperative for the believer to be strong in spirit, to overcome the relentless attacks of the world, the flesh and the devil. Paul, the apostle, commanded the Ephesian believers to be 'Strong in the Lord'. How does one do that? He is not talking about our physical muscles. It is in the working out of our spirit man that we can truly be strong.

This book will unveil the secrets of spiritual strength and the consequences of having a weak spirit, such as:

- The stronger you are in your spirit, the more miracles and breakthroughs you will experience.
- The stronger you are in your spirit, the easier it will be for you to resist the attacks of the devil.
- The stronger you are in your spirit, the healthier you will be in your body.
- The stronger you are in your spirit, the less influence the world will have over you.

Further books by Dr Glenn Arekion...

Available online at glennarekion.org
Download eBooks and MP3 messages instantly

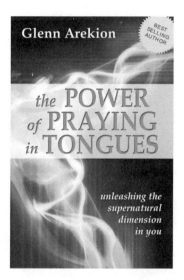

Are you ready for the supernatural?

Tired of mundane, dead Christianity and want to see Bible days in your life? Then this book is for you!

"I thank my God, I speak with tongues more than ye all" (1 Corinthians 14:18). Paul, the greatest apostle who ever lived, who wrote close to two-thirds of the New Testament and gave you your foundations for living an effective Christian life, uttered these words.
This founding father of the faith deemed "praying in tongues" of utmost importance and was grateful that he partook of such a great blessing.

Prayer is a command and calling of God. The Lord Jesus Christ specifically mentioned that His house is to be the house of prayer.
If you are born again, then you form part of the family of God, and prayer is your calling.

In The Power of Praying in Tongues, you will learn:

- The importance of praying in tongues
- Sixty expository benefits of praying in tongues
- The roots of negativism concerning tongues
- To develop partnership with the Holy Spirit
- To tap into supernatural Christianity

Further books by Dr Glenn Arekion...

Available online at glennarekion.org
Download eBooks and MP3 messages instantly

Does the sight of blood scare you? Make you shudder? Cause you to feel faint?

A childhood experience left Dr Glenn feeling this way for years – until he focused on the "precious blood of Christ" that provides eternal life and love.

Throughout time, the world has searched for the keys of protection and redemption. Every type of ritual, performance, and self-abasement imaginable has been attempted in this search while the true key has been overlooked.

The much neglected and noticeably overlooked subject of the blood of Christ trickling down the cross, which held captive His out-of-joint but unbroken body, is the answer that all of mankind has been waiting for. There are inexhaustible benefits of this uncommon blood; but before we can ever experience these benefits, we must first not only acknowledge them but also explore their possibilities.

This blood holds within it manifold blessings because of the covenant which it represents, whether it is approached for the salvation of a loved one, forgiveness of sin, or when the storms of life come upon us. This book will show you a step-by-step process to the victory in life that the precious blood of Christ holds. May Heaven kiss you and grant you its favor as you dig deeply into these anointed words.

Further books by Dr Glenn Arekion...

Available online at glennarekion.org
Download eBooks and MP3 messages instantly

What you are about to read will revolutionize your life and take you to a higher dimension! The anointing is the most indispensable force in the life of the believer. With it, you will have the power and faith to do great exploits. Without it, life and ministry will be a constant source of frustration and irritation. Many have visions but simply do not know how to make the realities in their lives.

This book is full of answers to your most frustrating questions. The name of the game is results, and when you know how to purposely tap into the anointing and treasure of God, you will:

- Be transformed into a different person
- Be elevated into a new place in God
- Be the catalyst for positive change in the lives of suffering people
- See your dream become your destiny

Seven ways to increase your anointing will answer your heart's cry. It will show you how to remove the powerlessness and lack of influence in your life, while empowering you to do the mighty works of God.

Further books by Dr Glenn Arekion...

Available online at glennarekion.org
Download eBooks and MP3 messages instantly

Jesus declared that healing is the children's bread. It is the divine right of every believer to walk in divine healing, divine health and divine life. However, as long as there are questions in your mind as to whether or not it is God's will to heal, your faith will be hampered from receiving what Jesus legally purchased for you.

Since Jesus Christ is the same yesterday, today and forever, He is still anointed to heal. The ministry of Jesus, today, is still a miraculous, healing ministry - as it was when he first walked the streets of Jerusalem and the shores of Galilee.

This book will answer the important healing questions and reveal God's thoughts towards your wellness. This book will eliminate doubts, banish fear and boost your faith to receive your inheritance. As you meditate upon the truths in these chapters, you will discover:

- Did healing pass away with the apostles?
- Is God glorified through sickness?
- Am I entitled to divine health in old age?
- How to resist sickness
- How to receive your healing
- 101 healing promises
- Daily healing confessions to cover your life

His Word is medicine to our flesh. He sent His Word and His Word healed them all. You are part of the "all" He sent his Word to heal. Receive your healing NOW!

Further books by Dr Glenn Arekion...

Available online at glennarekion.org
Download eBooks and MP3 messages instantly

The apostle Paul had an understanding of the new creation like no other authors of the New Testament. What was passed on in the first Adam is now passed away in the last Adam! A revelation of the new creation in Christ will revolutionize your life. New-creation realities will enable you to dominate the old creation, that is the old man. In this powerful book, Dr Glenn Arekion unveils the power of the new man over the old man and the mindset of Paul by the explanation of:

- The finished work of Christ
- The curse of the law
- The blessing of Abraham
- The believer's position
- The realities of the new creation

Break free from the fallen genetics of the first Adam passed down to the human race and live from your new identity in Christ. This book will enlighten your understanding to your position in Jesus Christ. No longer will you accept the lies of the devil as the norms in your life.

Enjoy your new status in Christ over all the works of the enemy and walk in victory.

Further books by Dr Glenn Arekion...

Available online at glennarekion.org
Download eBooks and MP3 messages instantly

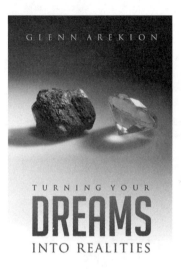

'I'm living the dream' is an expression that is often said but hardly ever experienced. Much has been said in the past years about the importance of dreams and visions for a fulfilled life and yet there are more dissatisfied people today than ever. This is because without wisdom, strategies and disciplines, visions remain grounded. Many have not reached the lofty positions that their dreams had for them due to a lack of these three fundamental forces.

Solomon, the most successful entrepreneurial king, knew the keys to success and he said in Ecclesiastes, 'For a dream cometh through the multitude of business...' Modern translations render this verse as, 'A dream comes through by much business, much activities and painful efforts.' Sitting down and merely having a dream without activities, strategies and certain disciplines implemented in your life will not trigger your dream to materialize.

This book explains the necessary wisdom strategies and the corresponding disciplines that you need to turn your dreams into realities. In this book you will learn:

- You are the number one enterprise that you need to build
- To destroy the excuses people use to abort their destiny
- The values of goals and diversities of goals
- Time management
- The ten characteristics of the diligent
- The million dollar habits you need to develop
- Wisdom secrets from the ants, the conies, the locusts and the spiders
- To turn your dreams into realities

Further books by Dr Glenn Arekion...

Available online at glennarekion.org

Download eBooks and MP3 messages instantly

Whatever is troubling you is not troubling God. Whatever is disturbing you is certainly not disturbing God. Why? Because God knows what to do about your problem. The reason you are perturbed and troubled is due to the fact that you do not know what God knows. If you knew what he knew then you would be just like God: cool, calm and collected.

Having access to the voice of God is the right of every believer. He wants to speak to you.

In this powerful book, you will discover the secret of receiving direction from above. You will learn:

- How God speaks
- Why 'fleece' is not for the New Testament believer
- How God led the apostle Paul
- How to fine-tune your spirit man to pick up on the voice of God

This powerful book will change your life.

Further books by Dr Glenn Arekion...

Available online at glennarekion.org
Download eBooks and MP3 messages instantly

You are only as effective as the quality of the information you receive. As a believer, you will be empowered, enlightened and energized as the exciting truths become alive in your heart and mind.

This book is a toolbox for the believer and minister, equipping them to fix life's problems. Life and ministry without the Holy Spirit, the Supernatural and His gifts will be a cycle of frustration but with Him actively involved, Bible results will become your reality!

If you are tired of living your Christian life without results then you need this great tool in your hands TODAY.

Through this book, Dr Glenn helps you:

- To develop your relationship with the greatest partner – The Holy Spirit
- To attract an active partnership with the Holy Spirit
- To grasp the purpose and validity of the gifts of the Spirit
- How to activate the gifts in your life and ministry
- To know what Paul meant by 'the best gift'
- To understand what the supernatural means
- To release the supernatural in your life and ministry
- To delve into 101 benefits of praying Tongues
- To understand the efficacy of fasting for a supernatural ministry
- To keep the fire of God burning in your life

This book contains 13 powerful chapters that will help you in your walk with God.